Common Faith, Common Culture:

HOW CHRISTIANITY DEFEATS PAGANISM

JOSEPH M. BIANCHI

SOLID GROUND CHRISTIAN BOOKS * VESTAVIA HILLS, ALABAMA

ISBN-10 1-59925-089-6 | ISBN-13 978-1-5992508-9-2
Common Faith, Common Culture: How Christianity Defeats Paganism.
© 2007, Joseph M. Bianchi. All Rights Reserved. Manufactured in the United States of America. No part of this publication may be reproduced in any form or by any electronic or mechanical means including information storage and retrieval systems without permissions in writing from the publisher, except by a reviewer, who may quote brief passages in a review.

Published by:
Solid Ground Christian Books
PO Box 660132
Vestavia Hills, AL 35266
205-443-0311

Visit our website at www.solid-ground-books.com
for information about our other publications.

11 10 09 08 07   5 4 3 2 1

"IN ACADEMIC AND NON-ACADEMIC CIRCLES THE NATURE, INFLUENCE, IMPORTANCE AND DEVELOPMENT OF CULTURE IS OFTEN DISCUSSED. Almost everyone recognizes the power that what is called *culture* has in the lives of individuals in both positive and negative ways. The question about what is the most productive and beneficial culture is hotly debated. In this book, Joseph M. Bianchi "asserts with boldness that there is one overriding and superior culture in the world." In so doing, he contrasts the pagan (unbiblical) concepts of culture with the biblical perspective. He then makes the claim "that Christianity transforms all other cultures for the good; that it has freed more people spiritually, intellectually, emotionally, and even literally, than any other movement in history." And he not only makes this claim, he also powerfully backs it up with solid evidence that this is so. *I commend this book to you and encourage you to buy it and then read it through at least twice and share it with others.*"

DR. WAYNE MACK, Pastor, Biblical Counselor, Conference Speaker and Author of *Your Family God's Way, Strengthening Your Marriage, Anger and Stress Management*, and a host of other well known books.

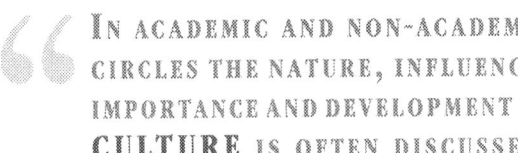

COMMON FAITH,

HOW CHRISTIANITY DEFEATS PAGANISM

COMMON CULTURE

CONTENTS

INTRODUCTION | 7

ONE—THE CULT OF CULTURE | 9

TWO—THE FALLEN CULTURE | 17

THREE—ROME: WHERE ANCIENT CULTURES MEET | 25

FOUR—FOURTH CENTURY—AND FORWARD! | 31

FIVE—PREVAILING CHURCH, PREVAILING CULTURE | 37

SIX—THE SHADOW OF ISLAM | 45

SEVEN—A CULTURAL REBIRTH | 57

EIGHT—LITERACY EDUCATION, REFORMATION STYLE | 65

NINE—THE PURITANS MAKE THEIR MARK | 75

TEN—THE WORLDLY PHILOSOPHERS MOUNT AN ASSAULT | 81

ELEVEN—THE EVANGELICAL SPIRIT OF REFORM | 87

TWELVE—A COUNTRY OF DESTINY | 91

THIRTEEN—THE RISE AND FALL OF GOVERNMENT SCHOOLING | 97

FOURTEEN—THE NEW PAGANISM | 105

FIFTEEN—MORE THAN CONQUERORS | 109

INTRODUCTION

IT IS NOT EASY IN THE MODERN WORLD we live in to define culture. With the advent of mass media, particularly the Internet, we can sit ensconced in our easy chair at home and imbibe on information pouring out of every news and information outlet from around the world. We thus share in a form of collective consciousness as never before in the history of the world.

The fact of the matter is, however, that all of us, from whatever country, ethnic group or tribe we come from, live in a culture. Anthropologists have grappled with the concept of culture for many years, but have failed to agree on what exactly defines culture. In the rather politically correct climate we live in these days, it is a very daring anthropologist who would even suggest that one culture is superior to another. They may use the term "different," or "variant"—but never "superior."

This book might be considered a bold step into the crossfire at this point, for it asserts with boldness that there is one overriding and superior culture in the world. It is a culture that transforms societies by transforming people one by one. It is a culture that, perhaps paradoxically, unites people from all cultures into one that shares a common goal and a common set of values. It is not a new culture, *per se*, but one that has been around now for over two thousand years: the Christian culture.

Our problem here begins, yet again, with first defining culture, and then making an argument for the superiority of Christian culture over, for lack of a better term, pagan culture. Over the course of the pages of this book we will attempt to do so. We will argue that Christianity transforms all other cultures for the good; that it has freed more people spiritually, intellectually, emotionally, and even literally, than any other movement in history.

For our purposes, we will define pagan culture as that which categorically rejects the redemptive teaching of the Bible, with its emphasis on the vicarious death of Christ in the place of sinners. Thus defined, pagan culture is much broader than simply those who worship nature, the elements or strange deities. While as a general rule we think of pagan cultures as technologically backward, such is not always the case. Indeed, even so-called "advanced" societies can lapse into paganism when secularism replaces traditional Christian worship.

Let us be clear from the beginning that Christianity, like all religions, is based on faith. In this case, faith in Jesus Christ, who came to die for those He would save. The old adage that "all roads lead to Rome"; that all religions are basically the same, have the same goals, and are trying simply to do "the good" does not play here. If we're going to make the bold assertion that Christian culture is superior to all other cultures, we must also assert that Christianity is superior to all other religions; another attack on the politically correct notions of our day.

We take this journey of discovery, a journey that may inform many, whilst angering many more. But we live in a very dangerous world, a world that seemingly has lost its moral and spiritual compass, and we need a direction, a safe haven, if you will, to sail toward. The finished work of Christ at Calvary and the Bible have provided this haven for over twenty centuries amid calamities, wars, revolutions—and every other trial the human race has endured. It is with this confidence that we prepare our ship and set sail.

ONE
The Cult Of Culture

When we ask "What is culture?" we find ourselves dealing with a concept that has as many answers as there are people groups. The definitions given us by many contemporary anthropologists simply leave one tongue tied as they attempt to give an explanation that will seem fair to all—and not offend any. This, of course, is a prescription for failure. Namely, trying to please everyone.

Despite this, there are some points of agreement. A perhaps loose definition of culture that we might all agree on would go something like this: The collective mores, traditions, symbols and values that define a people. Certainly as human beings we all share in certain things, albeit at different levels of intensity. For example, we may all love our families whether we are from America, Europe, Africa or the Orient. Yet, your particular culture may have a higher view of women than some others, or you may prefer a male child to a female child. In many cultures, monogamy is venerated, while in others having a mistress is, if not completely acceptable, tolerated. So we see that what one believes is good, bad or acceptable is defined by culture. This being the case, is any culture superior to another? Are one culture's values to be set apart as an example of that which another should attain to?

These are interesting and compelling questions. To make things more complicated, anthropologists sometimes refer to the "Inward" and "Outward" culture. The "Inward" culture being the shared mores, taboos, laws and cumulative sense of what is right and wrong; while the "Outward" reflects the "Inward": art, music, architecture, etc.

Within culture there are expectations as to how one is to behave in public, within the family, in the place of worship, within marriage, with the children; and toward those not of the same culture. Our natural inclination is to please the prevailing culture; to do that which would gain the approval of the most people wherever we live.

It is interesting to note that even so-called "counter cultures" produce a set of expectations that those within the particular counter culture are all too happy to adhere to. For example, during the Sixties, men grew their hair long to show that they were somehow different than "The Establishment," the ruling cultural norm of the day. They then turned around and "required" that all members of the Sixties' counter culture have long hair also. There may not have been a written manifesto regarding hair length, but everybody who moved in those circles knew what the rules were. Along with long hair was the drug culture. Smoking pot or taking LSD was an indication that somebody was "one of us." Thus counter cultures, in their attempt to be different, establish their own cultures with their own set of rules. In so doing, there is "sameness" among the counter culture inductees.

The Sixties gave birth to what is commonly called "Pop Culture." Popular culture is also hard to define. There are within it all the things that make up the common culture, but they are somehow homogenized and brought down to the lowest common denominator. This would include music, television, movies, and to a lesser extent, art and literature. These days, technology plays a big part in pop culture: cell phones, CD and DVD players, high grade video cards for PC gaming, and of course the ever popular mp3. One peculiarity of popular culture is its omnipresence; no matter where you go, you are confronted with it in various forms: on billboard ads, in radio and TV broadcasts, on tee shirts proclaiming the latest popular phrase, or from the latest in-vogue recording artist.

It must be said that this "type" of culture is distinctively western, in particular, American. American popular culture is a child of the

Fifties and Sixties. It has spread mostly due to rock music, a form of déclassé art that has been so eagerly consumed by the rest of the world as to have transplanted a bit of America like a seedling. Of course, there are other cultures that resist this invasion, particularly those that are heavily Islamic. Nevertheless, it cannot be denied that popular culture is, well, popular, because it is entertainment oriented. Increasingly our world desires entertainment above just about everything else. Even in countries that were once considered "backward," movies, music and television reign.

So, indeed, there has been, to some degree, an homogenization of culture worldwide. In actuality, however, this homogenization is only skin deep; despite the influx of other cultural ideas, individual cultures maintain their tried and true traditions, if not in actual practice, then certainly cerebrally. A particular culture may share some of its cherished values with another culture, yet there may be other things that they hold dear that the other culture finds abhorrent.

Holding certain things in common does not mean that cultures will not clash. When they do, our instinct is to simply chalk it up to "cultural differences" without making any value judgments. But, can there truly be a superior culture, one that has a value system that is quantifiably better than others? If so, how would we arrive at this position?

In order to answer this question, we must first start with what is common in most cultures and work backward. That is, *why* do these cultures have certain values in common, and from *where* did they get this concept that certain values are important (e.g., marriage, the idea that killing the innocent is wrong, education; as well as worshipping a deity)? We may also ask a further general question: Where did the concept of *law* come from? Is it an emanation of something innate in the human species, or is it of divine origin? And if it is of divine origin, what is the nature of the deity that created it or, more to the point, *which* deity created it?

It is interesting to note that even "myths" are shared by many cultures. A commonality among worldwide cultures is the story of a Great Flood, specifically, one like that found in the book of Genesis; a universal flood of divine origin that destroyed the ancient culture, and from which a small group of people were saved in order to start a new civilization.

For example, the Algonquin Indians told the story of the Great Serpent, Maskanako, who fought with the men of the earth after they became evil. The serpent brought great floodwaters upon the entire earth. After the flood subsided, the evil was "washed away." The Assyrians believed that the gods came together and decided to destroy humanity, but one of the gods warned an earthling who then built a large boat in which he loaded "the seed of all living creatures." The floods came and the boat landed on the top of a mountain. Seven days later the floods receded and the human who built the boat was granted immortality. The ancient Chinese believed that the god Gong Gong caused a twenty-two year flood to come upon all the earth until a hero dammed up the water with soil from heaven.

The question asked by anthropologists and liberal theologians alike is: Did the Genesis account evolve from a redaction of the various other Great Flood stories, or are the other stories an echo of the true, historical account of Genesis? Invariably, those who do not have a biblically-based faith will side with the "redaction account"; that is, the editing or knitting together of the other accounts to produce what they would say is western civilization's "Great Myth": The Genesis flood account. They may point to the fact that many of the other flood accounts pre-date the biblical scriptures.

The Christian believer, however, recognizes that the Genesis flood is a true historical account of God's wrath upon mankind's sin, and sees in the other flood accounts proof that God has placed in the hearts of men and women a knowledge of the truth of the Bible, which they will fiercely deny until, or if, they are converted. Moreover, the believing Christian looks around his or her world and sees that each country has a set of laws. These laws may differ from country to country, but all countries have a concept of law. To the Christian, these laws are simply echoes of God's will, for He is the great Law Giver. In particular, the Christian would see the Ten Commandments as the basis for all law. Thus, human civilization, no matter how faulty, is an extension of the divine will.

The Christian sees human civilization as waiting to be redeemed.

Wherever Christianity has taken hold, the rule of law, or at least a more humane rule of law, has also blossomed. Wherever Christianity has become the majority religion, more societal order has come, more concern for the less fortunate has increased; and prosperity is more likely. Conversely, where pagan religions dominate, superstition usually runs rampant, social order is less apparent, and modern science and industry are scarce.

The entire development of North America can be traced to Christians desiring to practice their religion in peace. True, many of these people were fleeing governments who also claimed to be "Christian." Nevertheless, the impetuses to create, build, establish law and develop government came from a deep religious faith—Christian faith. While other religions may have set similar goals, history shows again and again that it is Christianity that reaches the highest common good.

The industrial revolution did not start in the Sub Sahara, India, Indonesia, etc. It started in Europe, which had a solid foundation of Christian belief. Likewise, the Renaissance, the "rebirth" if you will, of civilization years earlier was a particularly European event. Is this so-called "Euro-centric approach" bigoted in some way? Certainly not, for it is based on the established facts of history. It is a simple fact that the great ideas, inventions and institutions emanated from the European continent. It is also a fact that many of the great men who are responsible for the aforementioned were themselves devout Christian men (e.g., Newton, Galileo, etc.).

As missionaries were sent to the various lands to convert the heathen (and we make no apologies for this term), the converts and the lands in which they dwelt changed both intangibly and tangibly. Intangibly, in that individuals were now partakers in the Kingdom of God, saved from the wrath of a perfect and just Creator; and tangibly, in that their culture began to reflect the basics of biblical law. Of course, this does not mean that all the land in which Christianity was introduced became mirror images of European society, but, certainly, they began to share common values; compassionate values that began to slowly transform their pagan societies. It would not be a stretch to say that Christianity is the most progressive movement the world has ever known. We refer not only to the improvement of economic conditions, but also to other issues such as the status of women.

We hear so much today about the "liberation" of women. Most of the voices chanting this phrase come from the political left. The liberation that they seek is one from what they consider oppressive "traditional roles": read, "wife and mother."

In the pre-Christian era, however, women in most cultures were considered little more than chattel, to be done with as the father, husband or society deemed fit, which usually meant having not much of a life at all. The introduction of Christianity began to radically change this. Christianity taught the profound value of each life, and the dignity of women. Rather than teaching to abuse or oppress women, Christianity taught men to "…love your wives as Christ also loved the church and gave himself for her…" (Ephesians 5:25, NASB). A heady and revolutionary thought today, let alone in the ancient world!

One could easily see how this type of thinking would shake a culture, for the good, to its very foundations. Yet, in today's world, Christianity is often scorned for having, as some would see it, an atavistic attitude toward women. The problem is not Christianity, but the paganistic cultural patterns that have become the norm. This is especially true since there seems to be a resurgence of interest in "goddess" religions and "earth-centered" faiths like Wicca (the so-called "good witch" religion). The exaltation of the *Anima*, or Jungian female soul-image of man, has been a subtle, but deadly force in the forging of the "new woman"; one that "can do it all" and does not necessarily "need a man." The apotheosis of this is the surge in Lesbian couples wanting to have children via *in vitro* fertilization.

The cultural norm, however, is one man, one woman, united until death. There was once an understood cultural mental image one would get when the word "norm" was used. Admittedly, the constant assault and drumbeat to dismantle what was once the standard has been quite successful. Thus, these days, to speak of the "norm" means to speak of something that is entirely relative and fluid, and which could change from year to year, or perhaps even month to month, depending on whatever social wind is blowing.

This begs the question yet again, "Who created culture?" The secular anthropologist would answer that culture is an outgrowth of man's evolutionary development; a by-product of the evolutionary process, if you will. The Christian would rejoin: "No! Man was created by God. God created Man in His image, and has set down expectations as to how we are to behave toward God and each other. Moreover, He has set down laws, social norms and principles to live by. It is either God's law or natural law; the law of the jungle."

So here is the great cultural divide: the secularist vs. people of faith, in particular Christian faith. For two thousand years the Faithful of Christ have staked their claim in a hostile world, and provided it with, as we shall see, an unparalleled standard.

TWO
The Fallen Culture

IT TAKES HUMAN BEINGS TO MAKE A CULTURE. This is perhaps an obvious and trite statement. The fact of the matter, however, is that if we are going to examine culture we must know the basic nature of men and women. Certainly, if we are going to be honest in trying to decide if one culture is superior to another we must ask an age-old question: Are men and women basically good, or basically evil? This question is germane to our study because secular anthropologists and believing Christians disagree on the starting point of the discussion.

The secular world views men and women as basically "good." They come into the world as a *tabla rasa*, a blank slate, upon which the prevailing culture writes and imprints its values. Since it is assumed that humanity has a total "free will," an individual can choose to do "the good," or hold "good values" as opposed to "poor values." Once again, the problem with this line of thinking is that it degenerates into relativism: who decides what is "good"? In certain cultures a new-born child is killed if it is not the sex that the parents prefer. Is this good? Closer to home, since the landmark court case of *Roe v. Wade* made abortion legal in the United States, over thirty five million babies have been "terminated." The secularist claims that the fourth amendment to the Constitution guarantees the right to privacy, and thus the right for a pregnant woman to decide whether she will give birth, or "end" the pregnancy. Right or wrong?

Christians are at odds with this worldview since they believe men and women are special creations of God. Therefore, it is God who establishes values, as we stated in the previous chapter. But there is more to the story.

The Christian presupposition is that the world in which we live is a fallen one. It is fallen in that it is not in the state of harmony and perfection that it once was. Of course, this view is diametrically opposed by secularists, who maintain that our present world is a result of millions of years of evolution, of natural processes that have forged, not only the physical earth, but also *homo sapiens,* humans, as we know them today. However, if man is a special creation, then there must be an explanation as to why the world *is* the way it is today. Otherwise, we might surmise that the God of creation is the "cruel scientist" that many philosophers have spoken of, chuckling in his laboratory while misery and chaos reign here on earth.

If we are simply a composite of our evolutionary past, where does "conscience" come from? Note that we said "conscience," not "consciousness." Animals are *conscious* beings, but do not possess a *conscience*. The Bible, however, talks about man being "in the image of God" (Genesis 1:26). Simply put, this means that man is a rational being, able to think, create and will. It does not mean that man has the incommunicable attributes of God; (i.e., omniscience, omnipotence, or that he can create things *ex nihilo*, "out of nothing"), but it does mean that man can have dominion over his environment, as well as enjoy a relationship with the Creator.

Man is a "living being" (Genesis 2:7), and as such he was created not only to enjoy the Creator and the created order, but also to work. Many view the Garden of Eden as a place where the first man, Adam, enjoyed earthly delights, void of labor. But this does not square with the biblical account. Man was to "tend and keep" the garden (Genesis 2:15); he was to work. As such, he had dominion over his environment. Yet, he lacked one thing: a suitable helper.

God declared that it was "not good that man should be alone" (Genesis 2:18), so He caused a "deep sleep" to fall upon Adam. Most people at this point are familiar with the "rib story"; God took one of Adam's rib's from which he formed "woman"—called such because "she was taken out of man" (Genesis 2:23). We now have the first human couple. God's instruction to Adam was quite clear: he could eat of any fruit of the garden, except for "the tree of the knowledge of good and evil" (Genesis 2:16). "Good and Evil" are opposites, and thus represent an unlimited wealth of knowledge, a most dangerous commodity, for it would mean that man would be autonomous, thus breaking his relationship with the Creator.

When Satan comes to tempt the woman, it is often said that he tells her the "ultimate lie": That God has forbidden the fruit because partaking of it would "open her (their) eyes" and that she would be "like God, knowing good and evil." The curious, and most dangerous, thing about Satan's attack is that it contains partial truth—not total falsehood. Yes, they would not immediately die physically, and, yes, they would be like God because they would now have a conscience that knows good and evil. However, Satan twisted the meaning of the partaking of the fruit: while the first couple would be "like God" and not *immediately* die, they *would not* have the omniscience of God and they *would* "die" spiritually. That is, their perfect fellowship with God would be broken.

When Adam and Eve partook of the fruit, that act of rebellion brought both the wrath of God, and His merciful plan of redemption. God pronounces a "curse" on all three parties involved: Adam, Eve and the Serpent (the Devil). The Serpent will be "cursed above all cattle...On your belly you shall go..." (Genesis 3:14). The woman will have pain in child bearing (v.16), and the man will toil by the sweat of his brow because "cursed is the ground because of you..." (v.17).

However, in the midst of this God makes a promise. While cursing the Serpent, God says, "And I will put enmity between you and the woman, between your seed and her seed. He shall bruise you on the head, and you shall bruise him on the heel" (v.15). Here we have the promise that God would send Messiah, a Savior, to redeem mankind. This verse is often called the *protoevangelium;* i.e., the "first gospel," because it is the first mention of God's redemptive plan.

The result of all this is that creation has now "fallen"; it is not in its original intended state, and is in need of redemption. The cascading effect of this is that all human events, and even the earth itself, are out of sync with the perfect will of God. Sin has entered the world, and along with it death (cf. Romans 5:12ff). Human events, actions and intellectual cogitations, will now have the unmistakable mark of the Fall. This mark will manifest itself as rebellion against God and His order, resulting in murder, evil deeds, evil thoughts, misjudgments—and the general downward slide of culture. You may ask, "If there were only the man and the woman in the garden, how could we speak of a cultural slide after the fall? Was there a culture in the garden?" Indeed there was! We mentioned earlier that there are important questions every individual needs to ask themselves, but especially the skeptic. We said they must ask questions like, "Where did the idea of law come from? From *whom* did it come?" Therefore, we might just as soon ask the question: "Where did culture come from?" For those who believe in the truth of the Bible the answer is simple: "God created culture."

This may beg yet another question: "What culture?"

The answer to this question is found in the original created state. God created man to live in harmony with Him; He provided a beautiful environment to live in, a companion to share his life with—and His direct presence to commune with. When God created the earth and all that is in it, he pronounced it "good"—and even "very good" (Genesis 1:31). Therefore, we are to look at the original state in order to grasp what God had intended for man. Certainly, we can never expect culture to reach what it was in the garden prior to man's fall. However, since right from the beginning of creation—indeed eons before the beginning of creation—God purposed to save a people for Himself, we must match what we believe culture and society should be, with God's original intention. Because men and women are in a fallen state and incapable of redeeming themselves, spiritual and physical death are in order for humankind apart from the direct intervention of God, who provides spiritual life. Regarding this process, the Bible says the following:[1]

Ephesians 2:4-5 But God, being rich in mercy, because of His great love with which He loved us, even when we were dead in our transgressions, made us alive together with Christ (by grace you have been saved)...

It is important to note here that this passage does not have universal application. That is, God is not saying to man that He has applied spiritual life to all, for the focus of the passage is on the redeemed. Rather, Scripture is telling us that those who believe do so because of God's action, not their own.

God has a specific people in mind; the people of God—those who put their trust in Jesus Christ as Savior. The spiritual principles that Christians must live by make up a unique God-centered culture, a culture that cuts across all race and ethnic lines. Revelation 5:9 speaks directly to this when it declares that Christ has purchased with His blood men and women "from every tribe and tongue and people and nation." God has taken a cross section of fallen culture and redeemed it into a new and living culture that plays by His rules; men and women who are new creatures in Christ (cf. 2 Corinthians 5:17).

So there is a Christian culture made up of black people, white people, Asians and Middle Eastern groups, that all share a common bond. What is God doing here? He is re-creating the world one person at a time via personal conversion, and making those redeemed people into a unified group. Since this group of people have been called out of the fallen culture, and are now diametrically opposed to it, they are now the "superior culture" that we spoke of in our main thesis. Why so? Because they are seeking to fulfill God's intended created order here on earth: being in harmony with their Creator via Christ's substitutionary atonement, giving Him glory; and living in harmony with their fellow man.

In the Old Covenant, God had given to Moses the universal code of conduct, the *Decalogue*, better known as "The Ten Commandments"—or by its Hebrew designation, "The Ten Words." These commandments were to be the rule by which the Israelites would be marked out as God's people; the distinguishing feature that separated them from the pagan world.

In Deuteronomy 5 the commandments are stated to the people of Israel. In chapter 6, the reason for the Law is given. Note particularly, verse 2:

> *...so that you...might fear the Lord your God, to keep all His statutes and His commandments, which I commanded you, all the days of your life, and that your days may be prolonged.*

God insists on obedience to His statutes and commands. Any culture that violates God's commands is in opposition to Him. We must quickly note that the Law of Moses was never intended to save in and of itself; it was a shadow of the full redemptive work of Christ. However, contrary to what many well-intentioned Christians believe today, the Law has universal application; not that it saves, but rather is the standard that God expects, thus showing men and women their need of a Savior. Yet, the Law, rightly understood, is still binding, even on the Christian.

The Law's message is that God is holy, and that there is such a thing called sin to which humankind is held accountable. Without the operation of the Law in the hearts of men and women, we are simply left with natural law; law that comes solely from the intellect of man—the "law of the jungle."

The apostle Paul comments on the Law's operation in conjunction with the gospel in Romans 7:7 this way:

> *What shall we say then? Is the Law sin? May it never be! On the contrary, I would not have come to know sin except through the Law; for I would not have known about coveting if the Law had not said, "YOU SHALL NOT COVET."*

Paul is clearly telling us that men and women apart from the Law of God have no idea what sin is, and thus cannot have fellowship with their Creator; they are in an adversarial relationship with Him. To not acknowledge the Creator and His rules is to be His enemy; it means a humanistic approach that loves man and the world more than the One who created it:

James 4:4 You adulteresses, do you not know that friendship with the world is hostility toward God? Therefore whoever wishes to be a friend of the world makes himself an enemy of God.

This is a chilling admonition, is it not? The world separated from the Law and Christ is the actual enemy of God Almighty!

We can thus draw the conclusion that the various cultures of the world that do not follow the parameters of Scripture are an affront to God. This does not mean that there are not cultures that attempt to keep order and do the so-called "good." It does mean that most, if not all, human cultures fall short of God's expectations. The dilemma then is, "Who then meets the standard?" The answer: the redeemed Christians from various cultures and ethnic groups who make up the "people of God."

This is then the "culture" that should be held up as the benchmark of human conduct. Since all races and ethnic groups are included in this culture, it is insulated from any form of racism. Indeed, racism and ethnic superiority have no part in this culture. When we compare culture with culture, however, Christian culture is the only one that meets the criteria of God.

We have a contrasting example in Scripture of man's attempt to form one, unified culture apart from God. Genesis 11:1-9 gives us the account of the Tower of Babel. At that time, humankind all spoke the same language and was united in a similar cultural way. The text says, "as they journeyed east." Clearly, they were moving as one unit. During their journey they decide to build a city and a tower "whose top will reach into heaven." This is simply a Hebraic expression that means "exceedingly high."[2]

First, after the universal flood, God told the post-deluvians to repopulate the earth. Naturally, this would mean breaking up into family groups and heading in opposite directions so as to facilitate the even distribution of the population. So, immediately, we have a disobedient mindset.

Next, the fact that they wanted to establish a city was a way of thumbing their noses at God and saying, "We're not going anywhere!" Finally, the building of the tower means that they were establishing a cultus apart from the Living God. It is theorized that this tower may have been an astronomical observatory; a way of charting the stars to establish their own calendar and, perhaps more sinister, divine future events. This would be a direct attack on the sovereignty and supremacy of God.

Although an historic event, the Tower of Babel serves as a metaphor for man's self-will, and his ceaseless attempts at usurping God's authority. Thus, we see that left to himself, man will form a culture that is in opposition to God, and God's intended cultural norm. Tyranny reigns where God's divine laws are absent, and we should be quick to point out the examples that come to mind: the Khans, the Hitlers, the Stalins, etc., which have marched through history and have left blood and destruction in their wake.

On the other hand, the Christian culture teaches love, joy, peace, longsuffering, kindness, goodness, faithfulness, meekness and self-control—the fruit of the Spirit of God. Man cannot exist without hope, and the hope that Christianity gives is that change is always possible.

---

1 For a complete discussion of God's work in salvation and election, see my book *God Chose To Save: Why Man Cannot and Will Not Be Saved Apart From Election* (Evangelical Press, 2001).

2 Cf. also, *God Chose To Save*, p.33

THREE
Rome: Where Ancient Cultures Meet

It is impossible to discuss Christianity and its impact on culture apart from the Roman Empire. Ancient Rome was the focal point of culture for hundreds of years and represented the best and worst of what man could produce, culturally speaking. On the one hand was the debauched mentality of conquest, brutality and subjugation. On the other was the seed of republican rule, engineering brilliance, literature and art. Like all great empires, Rome had its highs and lows. The core of Rome's history dates from approximately 145 B.C. to 476 A.D.

To this day, historians study the incredible military might and tactics of the Roman legions. Rome's military conquered a vast swath of the world including northern Africa, the Middle East, and what would now be modern Europe.

For all its intellectual and military might, the Empire could not escape the ignorance and superstition of the human condition; indeed, Rome was awash in both.

Curiously, the pagan religions of the time followed two divergent paths: either they sought a way to live this present life in some form of stalwart manner, or they were obsessed with the afterlife. The first approach was a form of naturalism that basically said, "Life is difficult. We need to be stronger than life." The second a form of anti-materialism that said life is full of painful things, and indeed the human body suffers horribly in this life through disease and the aging process, and therefore, there is a better life in the hereafter. So the soul apart from the body was a good thing—a release from the tortures of life.

The concept of spirituality in the Roman world was often viewed as a case of genetics. Some people, it was thought, were born with a higher degree of spiritual perception than others. With this variation in spirituality came the corresponding range of superstition. It was not uncommon for many to be so bound up by superstitious fears that they were literally afraid to go outside their door—and this was a fear they lived with each and every day! Accordingly, each locale had its own set of deities, many related to these fears. Other deities were in charge of the elements, war and prosperity. Getting out of bed everyday was a horrific event, for one did not know what deity one had slighted the day before, or what one you would fail to appease in the new day. Thus, many went through an almost insane protocol in the morning: asking this god to protect them from their enemies, another to rain so that their crops grew, another to protect them from accidents or diseases; and then for good measure, maybe an animal sacrifice or two for those gods whose names they could not remember.

To be considered "religious" in Roman culture meant worshiping a literal pantheon of gods, with perhaps two or three being your "favorites." Somehow, all of this nonsense was bound up with being a "good Roman." Conversely, not worshipping the gods (plural) was an affront to the existing culture.

Many have the false impression that Christianity was the object of persecution by the Roman state because Christ was seen as a criminal or, worse, a seditionist. Actually, the main accusation against Christians was that they "did not worship the gods." That is, because Christianity's focus was Christ, Roman culture could not comprehend a religion based on only one God. As we said, to be religious in Roman culture was to worship many gods. Indeed, this was believed so fervently that Christians were actually called "atheists"!

Christianity incurred the ire of many because it offended the reigning culture; it did not follow the cultural norms of the day. It said that there was only one God, the True and Living God—and that only He deserves worship. Moreover, Jesus Christ was the Son of God; indeed, God Himself come to earth to die for the sins of men and women. We will not here broach the subject of the Trinity, for it was confusing enough for the average Roman just to comprehend that only one God was to be worshiped, and that Jesus was this God.

Since Rome was the capitol of the empire, it was a place where those involved in commerce from the outer reaches of the various provinces came to do business. In this way, although there were certain characteristics that united many as "Romans," various other cultures were streaming through Rome. What's more, Rome's engineering prowess proved to be a major factor in helping the spread of Christianity. The various Roman roads, some still in use to this day, provided the needed travel routes for evangelists to reach the outer most parts of the empire—and then some.

In an odd way, God used both Roman superstition and its engineering genius in early evangelism efforts. The incredible roadways were used by the first evangelists to easily travel the commerce routes, while the "signs and wonders" of the apostles and early evangelists were quickly seized upon by many as authenticating the truth of the Christian message.[1]

Of course, there were phony evangelists and con men also in the mix. Even so, their effect was minimal, even nonexistent, when one considers the incredible explosion of conversions. Christianity offered a release from the chains of superstition and the dread of everyday life; the "gods" were dethroned, and with them the fears and problems that they produced.

The early church historian Eusebius said that these first evangelists were so empowered by the Spirit of God that many pagans converted immediately. While the average Roman citizen was chained by superstitious beliefs in "miracles" and "signs," when the true article came via the apostles, they saw it for what it was: The truth, and the beginning of a new era.[2]

So intense were the conversions and efforts by the evangelists that exorcisms became commonplace. In fact, exorcists were rising to the rank of official church status during this period.

The simple fact of the matter was that Roman society was changing: it was being purged of its superstitions and its pagan practices. Indeed, the culture was being transformed. When persecution did come, it was a negative barometer of success. The more persecution, the more evangelistic success seemed to be on the way. If there was less persecution, a downslide in conversions usually followed.

We must mention here one of the most important factors in the transformation of Roman culture: the lives of the evangelists and new converts. The stories of the signs and wonders of the apostles had an immense impact on the population, but even more so were the changed lives of those that converted. Let us emphasize the word *changed*. It was obvious to all who saw them that these new Christians were a breed apart. They were not just affecting a new way of life; they were actually *living* a new way of life. To the brutish Roman skeptic, this really meant something. This was especially true since some of these skeptics felt that Jesus was nothing more than a cheap trickster; a snake oil salesman who went from town to town with his traveling sideshow looking to ensnare the ignorant. It did not help, either, that Jesus used the phrase, "fishers of men," which in the ancient world was a familiar saying meaning to "hook" or trick an unsuspecting victim.

Early Christian evangelism was eagerly welcomed by the suffering Roman lower classes, since Christianity taught the equality of all men before God. But converts were also being made of the upper classes; the well educated, highly placed members of society—and they exercised tremendous influence over those they came in contact with, winning converts among the *intelligentsia*.

So at all levels of Roman society, despite intense persecution, the Christian faith was advancing. This book is not a tome on Roman history, and we are in no way attempting to give a comprehensive view of the entirety of Christianity's relationship to it. Rather, since

Rome was central and seminal to the spread of Christianity, no work on Christian or pagan culture would be complete without at least an overview.

We leave this chapter with one more, brief historical note. While much is made of Constantine's conversion in 312 A.D., his influence on true Christianity is suspect. Many historians believe he was still worshipping other deities along with Christ, and that he simply saw Christianity as the wave of the future to be taken advantage of. Moreover, his newfound faith did not seem to lead him to place Christians in high government offices. Yet it cannot be denied that his *Edict of Milan* in 313 A.D. took the heat off Christian believers, and made Christianity equal, if not superior, to pagan religions in an official sense. The edict was essentially a joint one, observed by Constantine in the West, and Licinius in the East.

In its time period, it was nothing short of revolutionary:

When I, Constantine Augustus, as well as I, Licinius Augustus, fortunately met near Mediolanurn (Milan), and were considering everything that pertained to the public welfare and security, we thought, among other things which we saw would be for the good of many, those regulations pertaining to the reverence of the Divinity ought certainly to be made first, so that we might grant to the Christians and others full authority to observe that religion which each preferred; whence any Divinity whatsoever in the seat of the heavens may be propitious and kindly disposed to us and all who are placed under our rule. And thus by this wholesome counsel and most upright provision we thought to arrange that no one whatsoever should be denied the opportunity to give his heart to the observance of the Christian religion, of that religion which he should think best for himself, so that the Supreme Deity, to whose worship we freely yield our hearts may show in all things His usual favor and benevolence. Therefore, your Worship should know that it has pleased us to remove all conditions whatsoever, which were in the rescripts formerly given to you officially, concerning the Christians and now any one of these who wishes to observe Christian religion may do so freely and openly, without molestation. We thought it fit to commend these things most fully to your care that you may know that we have given to those Christians free and unrestricted opportunity of religious worship. When you see that this has been granted to them by us, your Worship will know that we have also conceded to other religions the right of open and free observance of their worship for the sake of the peace of our times, that each one may have the free opportunity to worship as he pleases; this regulation is made that we may not seem to detract from any dignity or any religion.

It is a matter of historical debate whether or not this edict was actually doing Christianity a favor in the long run, since becoming a Christian for many after it was issued was more a matter of fad than of faith. However, the true believers could now practice their faith without fear of bodily or economic harm. That, of course, was no small accomplishment.

1 Ramsey MacMullen, *Christianizing the Roman Empire* (New Haven: Yale University Press, 1984), Chap. 4

2 Ibid.

FOUR
Fourth Century—and Forward!

THE FOURTH CENTURY SAW A CONTINUATION of vigorous missionary activity. It was a period when many intellectuals were converted, Jerome and Augustine being the most familiar. This, however, did not mean that paganism died an easy death. Quite the contrary. Pagan practices were alive and well and even remained entrenched in many converts. For example, many Christians prayed by the tombs of famous martyrs thinking that God would more readily hear their prayers. But this was an aberration, not the norm.

Slowly but surely, due to rigorous teaching and more comprehensive study of the New Testament writings, the nascent Christian church shed its pagan cultural skin and began to codify its orthodox teachings. The various church councils were a theological battleground leading to the formulation of universal beliefs and practices of the faith.

Additionally, the fourth century saw the stabilization of the canon. While there was still peripheral debate as to what New Testament books should truly be accepted as canonical, the New Testament basically had a bow around it, and there was general agreement as to the books that were to be considered "inspired."

The agreement on the canon brought with it a new sense of purpose and unity in the universal church. Missionary efforts increased exponentially. Christianity advanced from the Middle East to Asia Minor, Macedonia, Greece, Illyria and Dalmatia.

Roman missionaries also had great success in Gaul and Spain. The Faith was on the move in a big way, and there seemed to be a great thirst for the Word throughout pagan society.

In the last chapter we alluded to the fact that the lives of the evangelists and other converts were making an impact on the pagan society around them due to the witness of their lives. Additionally, we said that Christianity gave a new, positive image of women, elevating them from property status to a whole, intelligent person who needs to be loved and cherished.

There was, however, another group of people that Christianity elevated: slaves. Slavery was the norm in the time of the early church—so was cruelty. While it is true that some slaves were beloved and treated as family members, the majority were treated with incredible viciousness and subjected to dehumanizing abuse. If Christianity did not immediately free the slaves, it certainly brought them hope. Christians showed love toward those in bonds, and the message of the Gospel gave them hope both in this life, and the life to come. This came as nothing short of a thunderbolt to the ancient world, where slaves were often beaten, or even killed, for a minor infraction.

The aforementioned is just a taste of the way that Christianity was transforming pagan society. Christianity had an aggressive quality that was making inroads into the realms of politics, social relationships, education and mores, like no other belief system in history—and it was doing it at an astounding rate.[1]

This aggressiveness started to manifest itself both in private teaching and in the public forum. Christian teachers, seeing that many converts were clinging to their pagan ways, began to boldly speak out against pagan practices, branding them as "mad," "loathsome" and "disgusting."[2] In so doing, these teachers were drawing a spiritual line in the sand, for both the Christian and the pagan. For the Christian, they were essentially telling them to beware of continuing in the practices of the present culture; that it was unfit behavior, indeed, an offense to God. To the pagan, it was even a more grave warning: "Your soul is in danger. Turn to the true and living God, or face an eternity in hell!"

In contrast to this stark warning, other Christian teachers were also making use of one of the most venerated disciplines in the Greco-Roman world: philosophy. While the New Testament texts did speak of vain philosophy (Colossians 2:8), Christian evangelists were retooling it to fit a new context and to counter pagan logic, dismantling it with their own methodology!

This historical fact runs counter to what many liberal theologians and historians have been saying for years; namely, that the early Christians cared little for intellectual pursuits, and taught that all literature apart from Scripture was "of the Devil."[3] Christians, however, now saw the world in a different light; it was not a mere creation of chance, or an amalgam of creative processes from the various gods of their day, but the Creation of the One, True and Living God, who was calling on all men and women to repent and believe upon Jesus Christ.

Thus, philosophy was revived and put into its proper context. It was not the main vehicle for the spread of the gospel—Scripture still was primary—but certainly it was used in an ancillary way to establish a rapport with the intellectuals of the time.

Christians carefully reassessed Aristotle, Plato and Plotinus. They then tried to forge many of the principles of these thinkers into the Christian context. It has always been a matter of debate among Christians whether this attempted marriage between ancient pagan philosophy and the message of the Gospel has borne good fruit, but it cannot be denied that the subject was approached with much intellectual rigor.[4]

The second half of the fourth century saw a major transformation of the Mediterranean culture from its pagan roots to a basically Christian community.

One work that made a profound contribution to this change was Augustine's *The Confessions*. It was an autobiographical tome of a "tortured soul" looking for the meaning of life while indulging in everything the world had to offer, until the time of his conversion. It was Augustine who first taught the doctrine of Original Sin. That is, every human being born into this world carries the sin of the first man, Adam, on their soul. No one, therefore, is born sinless or innocent.

Many, of course, resisted this teaching, but Augustine persisted with great intellectual vigor and, because of the great amount of biblical evidence behind it, the doctrine was, with some exceptions, universally embraced.

The fourth century also saw the rise of monasticism, a movement that sought to retreat from the world, thus avoiding the temptations therein. While the monastic movement has a history unto itself, we simply want to point to one of its positive aspects.

The early monasteries, while having their own particular problems, were in many instances bastions of learning and the repository of early Christian scholarship. In particular, the many original autographs of the New Testament were kept safe, as well as early theological tomes, so important to the early development of the church. While one may argue as to the theological basis for the creation of the monasteries, it cannot be denied that they played a pivotal role in the preservation and transmission of crucial, early church documents.

Obviously, left to the pagan culture of the time, these documents would certainly have disappeared, or been perverted to suit the pagan norms; or even falsified with hideous elements to frame believers with outrageous practices. However, the monasteries proved to be safe houses for the copious writings of the period, and much of the early church writings we enjoy today are the products of their libraries.

Christianity in this period, therefore, was a powerful and creative force despite its opponents—many of whom were from the ruling state.

While the Roman state was promoting pagans to high office in order to handle the growing threat of invading tribes, Christians were, at the same time, introducing these very same tribes to the Gospel. For example, John Chrysostom (his name meaning, "golden mouth") preached to the barbarous Goths. So successful was his evangelization efforts, that the Goths became the principle missionaries to other Germanic tribes. The Franks were also converted at this time, thus a large portion of what is now modern Europe was brought to the Faith.

The fourth century was a pivotal turning point in the spread of Christianity beyond the boundaries of the Middle East and Northern Africa. The world was waiting, and it did not have to wait long.

1 Ramsay MacMullen, *Christianity and Paganism in the Fourth and Eighth Centuries* (New Haven: Yale University Press, 1997), p.11

2 Ibid., p.13

3 Author MacMullen, it must be pointed out, takes the latter (liberal) view. In so doing he is in step with the scholarship on this matter of the past twenty-five years. Contra MacMullen, et al, those who became Christians during this period simply had a change in their *Weltanschauung*, and now saw the world as a special creation to be understood only through the lens of Scripture.

4 Actually, it would reach its apex in the thirteenth century with Thomas Aquinas' *Summa Theologica*.

FIVE
Prevailing Church, Prevailing Culture

THE CHURCH'S PROMINENCE AND POWER excelled in the Middle Ages. Former barbarous tribes and their leaders were converting to Christianity at an astounding rate. While it is true that many leaders of the time took the moniker of "Christian" simply to look moral in the eyes of their subjects, it is also true that they exercised the "hypocrisy that saves" in that they gave much money and food to the poor out of obligation.

At the head of the class of this wave of conversions were the Franks, whose influence on missionary activity in the late sixth century was robust. However, by the early seventh century the Frankish oligarchy was being threatened by an independent spirit among the nobles of the kingdom. The famed Pepin used his might and influence to try to stem this trend and bring the errant nobles back into the unified fold. An overt attempt, it was felt, to forcibly emphasize the Christian faith would strengthen the monarchy. The thinking was that a Christianized tribe—or noble for that matter—is a pacified one. Again, hypocrisy can save, even though the original intention can be questioned. Indeed, in this period there were many more genuine conversions then ever before in the kingdom.

The negative drawback of all this manifested itself as more political entanglements with the papacy. Nevertheless, missionaries who at one time struggled to survive were now brought under the royal sanction of the monarchy. This meant that their evangelistic efforts would be well funded and, yet again, the gospel would go forward in great power.

Another towering figure of this period, Charlemagne, had a tremendous impact on the Germanic tribes of the day. Under his watch, the rather wild and bellicose tribes were converted to Christianity. Moreover, these tribes began to reflect a metamorphosis in culture. Where once preparation for war and paganistic religious practices were the norm, the majority of Germanic tribes were now more concerned with Christian moral principles and the evolving concept of civil government.

It is true that there was a period when Charlemagne used coercion—and even force—to attempt to convert unruly barbarians under his charge. However, when revered Christian leaders intervened, this policy was quickly dispensed with.

To some this may all seem like a phantasm, but it is historically true. Under Charlemagne, Christian culture flourished. He made it a point to gather scholars of the faith together and to encourage their work. Of special note is Alcuin, one of the most erudite men of his day. His scholarship inspired others to preserve and copy extent works on a variety of subjects.

It is, yet again, important to mention here that the charge of anti-intellectualism often leveled at Christendom falls harmlessly to the ground in light of the progression of learning and pedagogy stimulated by the faith. Far from being the "simpletons" of myth and legend, Christians were at the forefront of ground-breaking scholarship.

The church prevailed because it was *coherent*. Its members acted as a community; they upheld each other when persecution came—and they shared what they had with each other. Christians were regarded, even by their enemies, as kind, generous and hospitable. Certainly, the Middle Ages were not a period marked by any of these positive attributes, but within the Christian community virtue was cherished and, even more so, expected.

This period of history, admittedly, conjures up images of the Roman church beginning to consolidate its power, and thus the bitter taste of corruption, greed and clerical abuse stays on the tongue of many secular historians, and even many Christians. But the external, organized church was not always the "heart" of the church and often times the positive examples and exemplary lives of believers were drowned out by the overt abuses of the organized church. While the organized church and the pagan society it coexisted with may have used people for their own agendas, Christians in their communities and private lives were giving their time, and even their lives, for the comfort and welfare of others—some of whom were strangers.

It is ironic that the Middle Ages saw a revival of ancient philosophy, for it was this very philosophy that Christianity answered. That is, the distant Platonic god was displaced by a personal, compassionate Savior, who condescended to men for the sake of their salvation. Yet, as we mentioned in the last chapter, many throughout the history of the church felt, erroneously, that Christ, Plato and Aristotle were somehow compatible or, more likely, were *able* to be compatible. That is not to say that many intellectuals lapsed into heresy, for great contributions were made to philosophic inquiry because of this revival. The point of the matter is that Christianity, far from being reactionary, was progressive—especially in the social and intellectual realm.

We stated that the monasteries were virtual safe houses for much of the intellectual inquiry of Medieval times. Because of this, the charge has been leveled that the church, while allowing intellectual activity to flower within itself, kept the proletariat in ignorance in order to carry out its goal of social domination. While there may be some truth to this—we say *may*—there certainly was a trickle down effect that benefited the populace.

Since the vast portions of people in the Middle Ages were illiterate, it was the church that formed the link between the well-educated gentry, and the laboring peasantry. News, information, community events, and such, were all centered on the church. This was especially true in rural areas where it took quite a while for news to be known. The church provided a nurturing environment, and it was here that many, in fact, learned to read. This, of course, is in direct contradiction to the notion that the church was the purveyor of abject superstition.

The Middle Ages were not as "dark" as many historians have made it seem. The cliché that learning, free inquiry and progressive church activity were non-existent during this period is simply without merit. Indeed, this canard has its genesis in historiography that starts with the premise that the church was "regressive," "oppressive"—and steeped in a fog of myth and alchemy.

A closer reading of history shows otherwise, and we should be quick to point out that there have been reform movements all through the history of the church. Of course, the culmination of such was the Reformation begun in 1517. But this does not negate the many reform movements that sprung up during the course of Church history.

Of particular note is the Carolingian Renaissance of the late eighth century. Again we must mention Charlemagne, Charles the Great, who created a court of intellectuals without peer. His determination to advance learning was intense and without restraint. He made sure that the scholarship of the monasteries was of the highest order. The fruits of this scholarship flowed down through the echelons of society: From the scholars to the various bishops; then to the abbots, the priests—and finally to the people in the pew.[1]

In the year 789, at the behest of Charles, church schools for children started to sprout throughout the kingdom in order to teach "psalms, notes, chants, computus [i.e., calendar computations, usually to compute the date of Easter], and grammar."[2] This the church did with joy. Again, this does not square with the data that many historians would present us with: that the church made a concerted effort to keep the people ignorant.

Bishop Theodulf of Orleans, whose hymn *Glory, Laud and Honor,* is still sung in churches today, allowed parish priests to send their relatives to any monastery in his bishopric in order to receive a classical education. This would be the equivalent of sending your brother, sister or cousin to Oxford or Harvard free of charge. After receiving their education, many of these students returned to their communities and taught others, principally reading and music.

There is no doubt that the tide of ignorance was turning and, naturally, this was forging a different type of culture that was more literate with a better appreciation for the arts.

Because of the aforementioned, it was only shortly thereafter that most of the recently converted barbarian tribes of the west took on a more civilized, even erudite, pose. Moreover, the Balkan tribes, who were most resistant to missionary activity, converted. It is, therefore, important to see the direct connection between the march of Christianity and the advance of culture.

Another example would be what was happening in the eastern churches. There, art and literature were held in the highest esteem. While illiteracy still reigned, the architecture and art of the cathedrals was helping to communicate the Gospel message. The eastern churches were characterized by ornate art, usually depicting scenes from the New Testament, and often in the proper sequence of events. Thus, when a worshipper came into the church, they were virtually surrounded by the Gospel played out in picture form. Even the most unlettered person could understand what the paintings were saying about the life of Christ. Needless to say, this had an impact upon conversions and, by logical extension, local culture.

Certainly, it was not the case that the entire culture of the time became urbane and decided to sip tea instead of preparing for conquest. It is true, however, that there were great leaps in learning as a direct result of Christian influence. Left to its pagan roots, Europe of the Middle Ages would have not only been far darker than we suspect, it most likely would not have progressed into the intellectual and scientific powerhouse that we call the Renaissance. The curiosity that lead to scientific discoveries, the creative genius of a Leonardo DiVinci or a Michelangelo; all were brought about by a desire to better know the God of the Bible—to get to know His universe and man's place in it.

Rather than keeping the gods at bay (paganism), or looking for God in rocks and tress (pantheism), Christianity was teaching people that there is a God who can be known through his Word, and that He desires men to examine His universe to see all its wonders, wonders that redound back to the Creator. When it came to advances in medicine, industry, art and civic life, it is no wonder that Europe had the handle.

Historians often sing the praises of the great ancient cultures of the Middle East or even Africa. Yet, it was the Renaissance and the Industrial Revolution of Europe that advanced culture forward; that make our present world accessible to all via technology; that has brought modern medicine to the point of almost miraculous cures—and that has blessed us with a form of government that, while far from perfect, is quite benign when compared to others.

The motivation of the great explorers to whom we owe much, was more than to discover new lands wherein they could exploit the natural resources, become wealthy—and immortalize themselves. Unfortunately, this is how they are often painted by current historians. Rather, many felt the call of God to discover new lands for His glory, and to bring the Gospel to the heathen. We are not trying to whitewash history here and deny that many injustices were done, or that personal gain was not an element in the minds of some. Overall, however, there was a spiritual motivation in those who left the safety of home, family and country. Many of these men were committed Christians with a strong sense of purpose, and an unshakable faith. No doubt, Columbus did not always treat the native peoples he met equitably, but he always insisted that the Gospel must be preached to them and, ultimately, Christianity was introduced to the New World.

The argument is always presented that the native peoples that were evangelized also suffered brutality at the hands of the people that were trying to "save" them, and would have been better off if they had been left to their own religious practices. This argument itself is paganistic. For to the Christian, a worship of anything other than the God of the Bible and His only Begotten Son, Jesus Christ, is damnable. While many groups today are concerned for the political and physical well-being of Third World people, few, save for pioneering Christians, are concerned for their soul, their eternal destiny—*and* their physical well-being. Witness the many hospitals built by Christian denominations or organizations. We do not see Wiccans, Animists, or modern day Druids racing to the aid of spiritually and physically suffering people!

The Christian believes that there is a responsibility to help the less fortunate, and to meet their needs at all levels. This is what set Christianity apart from the belief systems of paganism and what made it so very attractive to those lost in a very dark world. Christianity, even in our day, is still concerned with the physical welfare of the less fortunate. Whether it is food and clothing relief to victims of a natural disaster, medical supplies to those caught in a war zone, or simply emotional comfort to those grieving, Christians are there. It must be added that they do so at great personal risk and without regard to race, creed or color.

The world has always mocked the faith of believers whilst accepting their largesse readily.

The prevailing church was and is one that conquers with benevolence, intelligence and sensitivity. Against all odds, it has made an indelible, positive impression on our planet.

1 Margaret Deanesley, *A History of the Medieval Church, 590-1500* (New York: Methuen & Co., 1985), p.60

SIX
The Shadow of Islam

AT THIS POINT WE MUST TURN our discussion to the faith of Islam, Christianity's greatest competitor for souls. This is especially true if one is discussing Christianity and doing so with the express intent to show Christianity's superiority over pagan culture and religion. Indeed, in the early part of the twenty-first century Islam has become the focal point of media attention, and is by far the world's fastest growing religion.[1] No other religion is more negatively central to world affairs in its confluence with culture, politics, and practice than Islam. It is beyond the scope of this book to recount the intricacies of Islam or its entire history. Rather, we will simply attempt to point out its basic character and its interaction with Christianity.

The friction between Islam and Christianity is well known. This clash of religions, however, is a bit more than skin deep. Islam and Christianity have totally divergent theologies and worldviews. Historians and liberal theologians have tried in vain to create the notion that this conflict is just some kind of mild sibling rivalry; that the problems between these two world religions are a result of simply misinterpreting each other. Of course, this is not the case. It is true that Islam has never quite understood Christianity, though. Most of Islam's views of say, Mary, the mother of Jesus, are composites of unorthodox Christian teachings of the seventh century, the one in which Islam was founded. The Islamic teaching that "God cannot become a man" is also in direct opposition, of course, with the Incarnation. Islam also rejects the resurrection and the trinity. There can be no meeting of the minds here; somebody is wrong.

It has been said that Islam was a uniting force that brought Arabs together. There is, of course, truth to this. Arabs in the seventh century were considered thoroughly nomadic, with no sense of permanence—and certainly with no understanding of civil government or law.

It is interesting to note that in the centuries leading up to the founding of Islam, many Arabs were converted to Christianity, especially the Syrians. Christianity was making inroads into Arab culture, tying many to the mores and cultural values of the west, particularly to the remnants of Roman society. So the idea that Arabs were hopelessly lost in paganism until the dawn of Islam fails on two points. First, obviously, since Islam borrows and then perverts many of the teachings of the Old Testament, many Arabs had been exposed to the moral and legal concepts of the Bible. Second, Christian missionaries were making great efforts to reach them with the Gospel, and by extension, present them with western cultural values.

This illustrates why the degree of animosity between the two faiths was so intense. Christian missionaries were making every effort to reach the lost, and were well on their way to great successes in the Middle East and Arabian Peninsula when Islam was founded. Oddly enough, the two religions got along amicably at first, trading goods and services among commerce routes known in that region of the world. Yet, certainly, Christian leaders knew that this new religion was heretical and would vie for the minds and hearts of the people. What concerned them also was Islam's violent way of "evangelizing": conversion by the sword.

If there was one thing that truly separated these religions, it was their mode of converting the unbeliever. Christianity sought to work with the unconverted in the realm of reason, education and, most importantly, compassion. Islam sought conversion—or else!

The facts as to the beginnings of Islam are well known. In 610 A.D. Mohammed, a man who could neither read nor write, claimed he was "receiving" messages from God via the angel Gabriel. These messages were allegedly written down for him, at first on whatever could be found (i.e., rocks, pieces of clothing, etc.), and then eventually on parchments. They were then brought together into the holy book of Islam, the Koran. Mohammed first preached his messages in Mecca in 612, where he encountered so much opposition, that he fled to Medina in 622. This flight is known as the *Hegira*, or "migration." It marks a turning point in the history of Islam, for at Medina, his "word" started to be received. From that point on, Mohammed surrounded himself with followers who were willing—and even desirous—to die for the cause.

By the time of Mohammed's death in 632, Islam claimed that most of the Arabs of the Western Arabian Peninsula had been converted, either willingly or unwillingly, to the religion of Mohammed.[2]

Curiously, Mohammed did not feel that he had founded a new religion, but rather that he had the purest form of religion that began with the writings of the Old Testament. He also felt that he had created one banner under which all Arabs could march, and therefore united them in a common cause. Rather than completely transforming Arab culture, he kept most of the old traditions known to these nomadic people, including the most negative: solving problems by force.

Force would be the *modus operandi* in spreading Islam. This was truly "religion by the edge of the sword." Less than twenty years after Mohammed's death, the Muslim armies had taken large parts of what was once the Roman Empire.[3] Persia was also completely under their control.

Alexandria fell in 642, and the wealth of Egypt was now theirs, as well as all of Syria and Palestine. The confident Islamic armies now plowed their way into Tunisia—and increased their westward expansion.

One of the great mysteries of history is the precise reason why Islam spread so rapidly. One could argue that Arabs were waiting for their own "redeemer," and that, to them, Mohammed filled the bill. This still does not explain the amount of converts—and military conquests—in a relatively short period of time. Islam presented the Christianized world with a wild fire of zeal that simply would not be quenched with reason.

In the areas where Christians dominated, there was relative peace with other inhabitants that happened to be Muslim. The same could not be said in areas that were conquered by Muslims. There, Jews and Christians could not build synagogues or churches, and had to pay a "toll tax" simply for not being a Muslim. What's more, they were forbidden to attempt to convert any Muslim under penalty of death.

Yet, since the Muslims lacked the necessary skills in keeping a government going, most government structures in conquered territories were left in tact—and were staffed with Christian administrators! It was the Christian subjects in these territories that had the skills to keep the civil government running smoothly, and their knowledge and expertise were invaluable to their Muslin overlords.

It is imperative to note, therefore, that without concessions to Christians in these territories, *the burgeoning Islamic empire would have collapsed.* It is ironic that the very people the Muslims desired to conquer maintained their civil and economic systems.

We again must point to the Christianizing of the western world, particularly the Roman Empire, as a major factor in preserving order in what would be deemed civilized territories. There can be no doubt that Islamic conquered territories would have degenerated into chaos had not Christians brought their patience, meekness and ingenuity to the fore.

Meekness and patience should not however, be confused with

naïveté, for Christian apologists were busy at work chopping away at the foundations of Islam.

John of Damascus, an eighth century apologist, in his major work, *On Heresies*, calls Islam the "superstition of the Ishmaelites." He goes on to call Mohammed a "false prophet" and describes how this "prophet" perverted the teachings of the Old and New Testament. Of particular note, is that John quoted extensively from the Koran. This would clearly indicate that many Christian scholars had access to the Koran and were busy studying the document in depth.

The Christian world, having literate defenders, was at work trying to ward off this newfangled pagan religion; it proved to be a task of Herculean proportions. However, even in Spain where Islam had some of its greatest successes, there were those busy defending the faith. An anonymous eighth century work appeared there called, *Ysotoria de Mahomet*. In it, the author calls Mohammed a "son of darkness" who "stole the Christian teaching" and distorted it. The parallels with John of Damascus are startling. Even in the early stages of the expansion of Islam, Christian thinkers were "on" to this new religion's theological perversions; they saw the dark clouds coming and were attempting to sound the alarm.

Another one of the great ironies of Islamic expansion is that in the conquered territories, Christians were introducing Muslims to the great thinkers of western civilization. In particular, the teachings of Aristotle and Ptolemy were imbibed readily. One could speculate that even though Islamic occupation may have been quite oppressive, it would have been even more so had not Christians added some intellectual reflection to the mix.

One exception to this may have been the region of North Africa, where there was little interest in Roman culture and intellectual achievement to begin with. As a result, North African culture did not do well under Islamic occupation. Without the element of westernized cultural thinking and supernatural kindness found in Christianity, the culture of Islam descended into abject cruelty. When North African Christians took it upon themselves to witness the faith and show compassion for their occupiers, they were rewarded with public beheadings.

Despite this, Christians continued to show love toward Muslims. This even included Christian intellectuals who were busy writing scathing rebuttals to the Koran. The love of Christ, His work on the cross, and the need to see the unconverted enter the Kingdom of God were the driving forces that kept the Christian communities together and vital.

It would, of course, be inaccurate to say that the Christian communities in these conquered territories were not impacted by the extreme pressures put upon them. There were quite a few conversions from Christianity to Islam. One wonders, though, if these were conversions based on true conviction, or coerced by duress. In any event, these conversions made many Christian communities close the ranks even more, and propelled them to make greater efforts in getting the gospel to their occupiers.

To portray Muslims as simply ignorant tribesman would be an injustice also. In the realm of science, particularly mathematics, Muslim accomplishments were profound. Additionally, the world today still sees the influence of Islamic architecture. Despite all this, sustained intellectual inquiry was not a hallmark of Islam. The impulses of conquest, fanaticism and paranoia were more likely endemic, than steady, scholarly progress.

There is also an interesting debate among historians as to the influence of Islam on creating feudalism. The idea is that Islam's many conquests split the Roman Empire in two, forcing it back on itself, and making it return to a totally agrarian culture. This became inferior to what was seen as a vigorous Islamic trade economy.[4] This trade economy, however, was *slave driven*. Slaves were used to haul goods, build buildings and places of worship, and for domestic duties for the ruling class.

This is in stark contrast to the Christians of the era who sought, for the most part, to end slavery as a normal practice. It was, however, an essential part of the Islamic economy.

The Koran taught that one was to treat slaves with kindness, even giving them similar clothing to what the master had. However, it also taught that a master could have an inappropriate relationship with a female slave if he chose to. Islam even had a working structure of traders to be sure that the amount of slaves needed was indeed attained.[5] A Muslim could buy a slave on a three day trial period to see if the particular slave was up to the task, or if there were any hidden physical imperfections. On this last point, there was much chicanery; slave sellers would often do everything possible to mask physical imperfections. It was easy to "get one over" on a fellow Muslim since Islamic propriety forbade the slave buyer from examining the body of slaves—especially female ones—too closely. On this note, the hypocrisy becomes obvious: A Muslim man had to be careful not to offend in the purchase of a female slave, but would be allowed to do with her what he will after the purchase!

It is true that the Bible speaks of slavery also, and permitted the children of Israel to have slaves (Leviticus 25:44). However, the context is in the particularism of the Israelite nation, whom God had chosen for himself, and who had primacy over the other nations. The apostle Paul told slaves to listen and obey their masters (Ephesians 6:5), but he certainly was not telling Christians to purchase slaves for themselves. He also tells Philemon to accept back runaway slave Onesimus as a brother in Christ. Many would ask why Paul did not simply tell Philemon to release him, when it was his prerogative as an apostle to do so. But this is perhaps trying to read too much into the particular text at hand, not considering the sensibilities of the reader of Paul's letter, or the cultural context wherein he wrote. Nowhere does the New Testament tell believers that it is proper to own slaves. Indeed, it only tells us that we ourselves are to be "slaves to Christ" (Romans 1:1).

The culture of cruelty is a major facet of Islam. All religions carry the imprint of their founder, and this is especially true of the Muslim faith. Mohammed was particularly brutal with those with whom he disagreed. The fact that he employed professional executioners to do his bidding should be proof enough.[5] You can call the apostles a confused lot at times, and if you are an unbeliever you may call Jesus Christ "simply a man," but the clear teachings of the New Testament stand against the life of a man, Mohammed, who claimed to speak for God.

Jesus tells his followers to love their enemies, do good to those that persecute them, in order that Christians should be "sons of your Father in heaven" (Matthew 5:43-48). Jesus is therefore telling his followers to reflect the very nature of God the Father. Basically, he is telling them not to resist the persecutor, or the ungodly man, but to respond with supernatural kindness.

In contrast, Mohammed used the *suras* (i.e., the verses of the Koran that were allegedly given to him by God) as a form of protection against his enemies and those who did not agree with him. In doing so he was drawing attention to himself, a mere man. He could therefore make pronouncements that directly benefited him and simultaneously condemned his opponents. What would happen if we telescope this mentality into our day? How it would affect one's thinking regarding others and impact the culture wherein it is present?

Many modern Muslim countries have gone back to the *sharia*, or Islamic law, as the absolute law of the land (e.g., Sudan, Iran, and Pakistan). The effect has been social and economic stagnation. Meanwhile, the Christianized west has seen tremendous progress in the areas of technology, medicine and the arts. Of course, we add the qualification that much of so-called western culture these days is secularized. This is not due to the failure of the Christian faith, but the general retreat of the main-line churches over the past generation.

In the Muslim faith, *jihad,* or "holy war," is not just a concept held by a fanatical few that are hijacking a "wonderful world religion," but, rather, *the very essence of Islam.*[6]

Unlike Christ, Mohammed was a warrior, a man who *actually killed his enemies* and those that opposed him or did not believe his message. Compare this with the Jesus who stood before Pilate (cf. Matthew 27:1-26; Mark 15: 1-5; Luke 23:1-12). True to the very end, Jesus accepted His fate because it was the way that God the Father would redeem the world. Jesus was setting an example for His followers.

Likewise, so did Mohammed.

The followers of Islam through the ages have shown again and again that executions, murders and "holy war" are the only ways to deal with the unbeliever. When Christ said that He had come to bring a "sword" into the world (Matthew 10:34), He was referring to the controversies that would exist between believer and unbeliever, some of whom would be among a believer's own family. Jesus did not, however, tell his disciples to kill the infidel, or raise an army to do so in their place.

The question may be asked, "What about the Crusades?" Fair enough, but remember that as terrible as historians have made them, the Crusades were only embarked upon after the Muslim hordes had made their way into the outskirts of Europe! Spain was engulfed by the Moors, and it appeared that all of Europe was going to be overrun.

We do not want to put blanket exoneration on the Crusades. Nevertheless, historians have not dealt fairly with this period of Christian history. The Crusades were basically a defensive measure against an aggressive invader. All of Europe, essentially, would have fallen to the Mohammedan Empire. Based upon what we have said in this chapter, it would have been one of the greatest tragedies of history.

When Mohammed and his armies took over Medina, for example, he demanded that the Jewish Beni Qoreiga tribe immediately convert to Islam. Appalled by this overture, the Jews refused. They were then summarily beheaded publicly, eight hundred in all. Their wives and children were sold into slavery or used for the sexual gratification of Mohammed's army.

All this in the name of "the religion of peace."

There is an historical mystery that must sting the conscience of every Muslim. Just prior to his death, Mohammed called several of his top leaders to himself. He told them he would soon be receiving more messages from God which would be written down as *suras*. These *suras*, he told them, would be necessary in order to prevent the Islamic people from falling into grievous error that would put their souls in eternal danger. Mohammed died before he could dictate these "messages from God."

What were these messages to be? What error was he speaking of that could endanger the eternal soul of a Muslim? Was his conscience bothering him? We shall never know.

We do know that Christianity, in all its teachings, seeks to preserve life—even the life of its enemies. It teaches the sanctity of the unborn; the necessity of taking care of orphans and widows (James 1:27)—and an eternity for believers with their Lord, praising his great works (Revelation 5: 11-13).

The Koran teaches an eternity where celestial virgins will satisfy the every need of the faithful. If one believes in Allah, the question must be asked: "How does this glorify him?"

Most Muslims never hear about how the great Caliphs (i.e., those who became Muslim leaders after Mohammed's death) would characteristically have their own wife or children strangled if they felt their family members were not totally loyal, or if their offspring would try to usurp them.

Our current news is replete with stories of Muslim suicide bombers, who are lionized by Islamic terrorists throughout the world. But the typical Muslim child is never told that the Koran says:

[4.29] O you who believe! do not devour your property among yourselves falsely, except that it be trading by your mutual consent; and do not kill your people; surely Allah is Merciful to you.
[4.30] And whoever does this aggressively and unjustly, We will soon cast him into fire; and this is easy to Allah.

Thus, suicide—as well as killing other Muslims—is condemned! The inherent contradiction is nothing short of mind-bending.

No, the culture of Islam and the culture of Christianity cannot be reconciled. One is a culture of death, the other of life. Yet many Christians daily risk their lives to bring the Good News of Jesus Christ to Muslims, as well as to meet their physical needs.

Unfortunately, on every level possible, Islam is at war with the Christian faith as well as with all those who will not bow the knee to their god and prophet.

1 Richard Fletcher, *The Cross and the Crescent* (New York: Viking Press, 2003), p.11

2 Ibid., p.13

3 Ibid., p.61

4 Ronald Segal, *Islam's Black Slaves* (New York: Farrar, Straus and Giroux, 2001), pp. 35-39

5 Paul Fregosi, *Jihad* (Amherst, N.Y.: Prometheus Books, 1998), pp.46-47

6 Ibid., p.57

SEVEN
A Cultural Rebirth

THE PERIOD FROM THE TIME OF MOHAMMED until the beginning of the sixteenth century saw the ebb and flow of power emanating from the Church of Rome and the various Popes. It is difficult to speak of the "the church" in this period apart from the papacy. It is even more difficult to make the argument that as the papacy increased in power, the church was actually doing "the good," helping people—and culturally advancing society.

Although the papacy was a politically destructive force in this period, individual Christians, as well as quasi-reform movements within the Catholic Church, were busy doing the true will of their Savior, Jesus Christ. The pressure cooker of greed, doctrinal perversion and political intrigues that were embodied in the popes erupted into the Reformation, a movement that many still hold as the greatest of all historical events next, of course, to the birth of Christ.

It is important to understand that these times were not as horrible as many make them, nor as august as Catholic apologists would have us believe. But in spite of the many sinister episodes of this time in history, it served as a precursor to one of the greatest times in church history, and as a launching pad to a religious and cultural movement that would have universal impact.

Before we can speak of the Protestant Reformation, we must provide some kind of backdrop as to what was to unfold. Again, when we think of the reign of Charlemagne, we must keep in mind that he thought of himself as the preserver of the Roman Empire. Critics would agree, except that they would say that his leadership and administration was inferior; it was less sophisticated on every level. However, he would not yield on his concept of a united Europe under the banner of Christianity. On an economic level, when Charlemagne's rule broke down, feudalism began to be built up. We spoke earlier of Islam's hold on the major trade routes and its causative effect in the formation of feudalism. Europe under feudalism was a virtual tug of war between temporal rulers and the popes, who were attempting to claim the divine right of rule.

By the ninth century, the popes were actually beginning to have some successes in this regard. For example, Nicholas I crowned the emperor and presented him with a sword. This was a highly symbolic gesture indicating that the pope had not only power to bless, but to dictate policy as well. Pope John VIII went a bit further and declared the pope could not only crown the emperor, but *choose* him as well.

The waning empire was briefly revived under Charles the Fat, but Viking invaders plunged all of Europe into chaos. This is the "textbook" explanation of how feudalism came to Europe. Regardless of the explanation, with Europe in confusion, the papacy sank deeper and deeper into corruption—and even deeper into political intrigue. By the tenth century, however, the emperors were in control, not the popes.

Additionally, simony, or the selling of church offices, was the rule of the day. This meant that the church was basically being run by the laity. The odd effect of this was that those who truly cared for the church and the truth of Christianity were awakened, and the forces of reform began to gain momentum. Hope reached its zenith with the election of Nicholas II, who decreed that no temporal body could interfere with the election of a pope, an odd hypocrisy considering the popes meddling in secular affairs. This pope made it clear that only the cardinals could elect the pope. More important than this, he stood firmly behind the reform movements in the church.

Ironically, the rule over the Papal States increased. This elevated the prestige of the pope to new heights. Other changes were taking place also. The strong Byzantine influence over Rome faded, as did the resentment of the African church—always trouble spot in the world for popes.

By the twelfth century papal power was at its highest point. Even historians of our time, regardless of their perspective or theology, have called the medieval papacy one of the greatest formulations for the conduct of human life.[1]

It is an understatement to say that eventually the papacy would become diabolical in both its spiritual perversions and political machinations. Yet, the inculcation of general biblical values into the culture provided an intellectual paradigm that would stand against the Muslim onslaught, as well as the barbarian invaders.

With the election of Innocent III, the most intellectual pope of the Medieval period, the papacy made deeper inroads into the political life of Europe, reversing the aforementioned trend of the emperors. The positive outgrowth of this was an advancement of culture, whereby literacy was held up to the masses as a laudable goal. But the dark clouds of history were starting to descend upon Rome.

By the middle of the twelfth century force was being used against heretics. With absolutely no New Testament justification, the Roman church coerced, taunted—and executed—those whose theological views were in opposition to the Magisterium. The lack of critical interpretation of the Old Testament texts yielded a theology of retribution. Moreover, this period of European history saw the revival of Roman law, which required death for "heretics," specifically those perceived as disturbing the social order.

Meanwhile, the church structure was becoming more and more complex. Church territories were being divided into parishes governed by bishops who acted as legislators and judges. Thus did the church of Rome close its grip on the social reins of society. In the realm of worship, things were faring poorly. Where once the gathering of believers was a simple affair composed of the reading of scripture, a sermon and a communal meal, it now took on the accoutrements of pagan worship; the common man could no longer touch the communion bread as that was now the exclusive right of the priests and bishops. The worship was fenced in an area where there was a literal altar. The eventual codification of the doctrine of transubstantiation, whereby the bread and wine of communion were said to actually become the very body and blood of Christ, made the wall between laity and clergy high and insurmountable.

With the evolution of the Mass, worshippers became observers, rather than participants. The pomp and glory of the Mass could leave one simultaneously awestruck and alienated.

Considering these developments, how could one say that the church to any degree was a "superior culture"? Do superior cultures oppress and control? Do they wrest control of the social order to make it "better"? Do they interfere in government affairs and threaten politicians who do not do their bidding?

The answer certainly is, "No!" However, in a Medieval world, the sophistication of the organized church was to be preferred to the oftentimes incompetent feudal lords, who offered all the interference without the spiritual benefits. The church brought structure and order to Medieval life, and despite its errors, comfort to many. There is another historical benefit that cannot be overlooked: it prepared Europe intellectually for the Renaissance and the Reformation. At the least, the church gave the world a notion of the truth of God's Word as revealed in the Bible. In so doing, it served as a primer for those who would come years later and rescue the church from its abject theological errors.

So in a world where brutal barbarian invasions was a way of life, the church provided a "wagons in a circle" mentality, allowing the populace to feel, at least minimally, secure in their stark and difficult lives.

Like a giant ocean liner collecting barnacles as it goes, the Catholic Church increased its collection of questionable doctrines and canon laws. It may be argued by some that in its attempt to ferret out heretics and pagans that the church was adopting beliefs that were, in and of themselves, pagan (e.g., praying to the saints and the dead, the doctrine of purgatory, etc.). Eventually, these beliefs were to come into question and spark the greatest religious, and arguably historical, change in society—the Reformation.

Unfortunately, when history is taught in our universities today, the total impact of the Reformation is never fully realized. The mentality is that this was purely an historically interesting period for "religious" people, or religion in general. Little is taught about the incredible impact the Reformation had on society as a whole and how it intellectually changed the face of Europe.

With every historical change, there is usually the accompanying bloodshed. Certainly, the Reformation had its share, and regardless of theological persuasion, the guilt lies firmly on the shoulders of those who instigated it. Nevertheless, the men who were at the forefront of Reformation history stand as giants in the realm of societal advancement, and must be given their due.

Before we can look at the impact of the Reformation, however, we must first give a general overview of its precursor, the Renaissance, for it provided the foundational inquisitive spirit that endued the Reformers and their followers with a desire to seek truth. The Reformation, it must be kept in mind, was a *progressive* movement. Not in the sense that it sought to "contemporize" the Christianity of the time, but rather that it put effort into the necessary scholarly work to strip away the false Roman barnacles, and to defend the purity of doctrine as reveled in scripture, apart from the additions and modifications of men.

The Renaissance, or "rebirth," of Europe was centered in Italy. Thus, to talk of the Renaissance is to talk, primarily, of the history of Italy in the fourteenth, fifteenth and sixteenth centuries. We may look at Italy in this period as a prototype of what was to eventually become "modern Europe." For all its new inventions and artistic accomplishments, it wasn't the objective things that we associate with the Renaissance that made it what it was; it was the intellectual shifts that impacted the culture. Rather than something completely new, the Renaissance was a modification and a furthering of the classical mentality. Classical learning was revived, and with it a desire to learn the wisdom of the past. This may seem odd as we associate this period of history as a forward movement, which indeed it was, but perhaps it should be more properly termed an extrapolation that had more in common with the Middle Ages.

What was starting to emerge in the Europe of the Middle Ages was the idea of a common culture, a common ethnicity. The classical world, dominated by Rome, held that occupied territories were not to be alien to their conquerors, but were to be integrated into their culture. Despite the constant warfare of the Medieval period, Europe was beginning to see itself as a unified whole. Again, this may seem like a contradiction, for even Italy was not unified, but made up of city-states, independently governed—and often at each other's throat. But trade with other parts of the world made these city-states economic power houses. This newly acquired wealth had a revolutionary impact on the society. Where there was once the ruling nobility, and then the poor and destitute, trade and mercantilism started to produce a fledgling middle and upper class of bankers and merchants. More wealth produced more free time. Not being ones to be seen as ruthless money-grabbers and tyrants, both the nobility and the wealthier emergent merchant class became patrons of the arts and science, pouring money into the support of poets, sculptors, scholars—and those tinkering with new inventions, one of the hallmarks of this age.

The area of Italy known as Tuscany seemed to be an incubator of great writers and thinkers. This region produced men such as Dante, Machiavelli and Boccaccio.

What was happening in Italy soon spread to other parts of Europe. The world was now changing into a place where pure brute power was not enough, a world where diplomacy and political maneuvering behind the scenes became commonplace. Artisans, writers and thinkers were energized like never before. The genie of inquiry could not be put back in the bottle, and Europe was ablaze with new intellectual pursuits.

What made the landscape of Europe more complex at this time was the power increase in the Papal States; that is, those districts under the direct control of Rome. In our study so far, we have attempted to be as fair as possible with the established church. It would be unfair, and not historically accurate, to paint the Roman church as either a bastion of the faith, or completely in the camp of the devil. Rather, it became a product of the times, mixing good and evil. We are not saying that the Roman institution as it has come to us in our present age is the bearer of truth, but rather putting it in its time context during the Renaissance, it appeared to have some seemingly positive goals.

First, in the midst of shifting military and political alliances, it sought to keep the Christian world unified. Second, although containing some twisted doctrine of its own, it nevertheless beat down heresies that struck at the very deity of Christ. Lastly, it protected Christendom from the onslaught of Islam, mainly by driving the Ottoman Turks out of Europe.

This in no way exonerates the church from its brutal excesses or its extra-biblical doctrinal formulations, but it does give us a clearer view of the Catholic Church of this period, apart from pure partisan accusations or emotional diatribes. To be sure, the popes, caught up in the political labyrinth of Europe, themselves became, at times, nothing more than rank politicians, looking to advance their personal agendas.

Although currency had, to a certain extent, been in use in Europe, the demand for same meant that many Church projects would need a fresh influx of cash if they were to be sustained.

Doctrinally, the church taught that although one's sins could be forgiven by a priest, the temporal effects also had to be eradicated by good deeds; one had to suffer the consequences even if forgiven. Thus the church formulated the selling of indulgences, whereby a worshipper could pay to have these temporal punishments removed. From the church's point of view, it was a brilliant idea, for not only did it strengthen control over the laity, it raised money for the church's coffers.

With the risk of oversimplification, this one doctrine of indulgences was a ten ton block of TNT that was going to be ignited by an agitated Augustinian monk, and change the face of Europe—and the world—forever.

---

1 R.W. Southern, *Western Society and the Church in the Middle Ages* (Hammondsworth, UK: Penguin Books, 1970), p.105

EIGHT
Literacy Education—Reformation Style

The Protestant Reformation has had an irrefutable effect on world history. It is not an exaggeration to say that it was the seed from which the modern world—and the modern culture—grew. Although the Catholic Church was supreme at the time, forces were at work that would derail its grip.

For a young monk by the name of Martin Luther, the wholesale selling of indulgences was an act that, for him, was the last straw in an ever-growing skepticism with the decisions of the Roman church. By nailing his ninety five theses to the Wittenberg door, he essentially threw down the gauntlet, challenging Catholicism to prove it was indeed the "one true church." Luther did much more than simply challenge a doctrine; he challenged the notion that only the church (i.e., Catholic Church) could interpret the Bible.

The real debate, however, was in the realm of soteriology, or the "doctrine of salvation." That is, according to the Bible, how is a person saved; made right before God? Is it on the basis of the works that they do? Is it the church administering the sacraments that saves? The original idea of indulgences was formulated by a thirteenth century theologian, Alexander of Hales, who said that a "treasury of merit" existed. This was a "spiritual pool," if you will, of excess grace won by Christ on the cross and the good works of the saints. Only the church had the power to dip into this pool and dole out its graces to believers.

The proceeding attack upon this doctrine by Martin Luther and the other reformers had a very positive side effect: the beginning of Godly public education and a move to eradicate illiteracy.

Between the years 1517 to 1520, Luther produced no less than thirty publications, an absolute explosion of literary activity. Over the course of his life, he wrote more than four hundred fifty theses!

The printed word was powerful, but under the sure hands of the reformers, it became earth shaking. Mohammed had always referred to Christians as the "people of the book." Of course, this was true—and during the Reformation, this became especially true.

The amount of reading that occurred during the Reformation is absolutely unparalleled in the history of the world.[1] Even to our present day, no period of time has seen a greater production of wood carvings, pamphlets and books put to use in the army of a single cause. Just about every avenue of human communication flowered.

Eberlin Von Gunzburg was a convert to Protestantism by way of Luther's writings. Inspired by his mentor, he became a writer himself. In his famous fifteen pamphlets entitled, *Comrades*, he touched upon just about every social ill; from monasticism to political corruption, from the ineptness of Catholic leaders, to the ineptness of local secular governors. All the remedies he suggested to these ills were solidly biblical, and he not only developed a loyal following, but his suggestions were actually being implemented.

We see here how the Reformation's spirit of true biblical liberation leads to intellectual inquiry, and spiritual and social advancement. The pagan knows nothing of intellectual inquiry, except that it might increase his or her personal lot. For is not the heart and soul of a pagan bent toward self gain, accumulation of goods, power and egotism? We digress here a moment only to show the stark contrast between pagan activities and the Gospel. The unbeliever can never know true knowledge, but rather seeks the impaired knowledge of the world. Certainly, the reformers were men with sins and passions of their own, but their overriding desire was truth; the truth of the Word of God. This truth was no "pie in the sky" promise that never delivered, but a living faith that was able to transform men and women—and society.

Luther's writing was impacting every sector and every social strata of society. Hans Sach, a humble shoemaker turned poet, profoundly effected the German people with his work, even as he lauded Luther's reforms. Paul Speratus, a convert to Protestantism, wrote hymns that were not only beautiful, but doctrinally sound. Hence, the average person could sing hymns and learn theology at the same time.

Luther was seen as a man not only striving for biblical truth, but for the liberation of the intellect from its Medieval bondage. In this regard, Luther was also a social reformer. The genius of Luther is that his writing, although primarily interested in the grace of God as it pertains to the sinner, struck a cord deep in the heart of European men and women regarding their lives and the culture in which they moved. No longer would their mind be slaves to the Roman church, no longer would their consciences be captive to superstitions that entrapped their souls.

The love of books and learning was rising like a giant tide, and the thirst for knowledge simply could not be quenched. Even though Luther was condemned as a heretic by the organized church, people were willing to risk all to read his writings, or to see or hear him.

All we need do is look at the enrollment numbers at the University of Wittenberg where Luther taught. In 1516 there were 162 students enrolled who were listening to Luther's lectures. By 1520, a mere four years later, that number had risen to 552. No doubt, Luther was gaining a following among the young *intelligentsia*.[2] Most famous, of course, was Melancthon, who came under Luther's influence. Melancthon had studied at Tubingen and Heidelberg, and received his M.A. in classic literature before the age of seventeen! He went on to become the principle author of the *Augsburg Confession*.

What many do not know is that Malancthon, inspired by his new evangelical faith, was one of the first true educational reformers. Under his guidance, many monasteries were turned into civic schools where reading and biblical instruction could take place. Following Malancthon's lead, Johannes Sturm was organizing city schools at Strasbourg.

Considering the aforementioned, it is an historic fact that the Reformation was directly responsible for the creation of public education. The education system the reformers created was a far cry from today's secular humanist enclave. For the reformers, all education must point back to God, the Creator of all things, and from whom all wisdom flows. Their emphasis on literacy was simply an outgrowth of their belief that the Bible be read and enjoyed by all people, freed from the shackles of Catholicism.

Clearly, the Reformation gave new meaning to people's lives. They were now spiritually renewed, and culturally aware. The playing field was being leveled; from the aristocrat to the lowliest peasant, all now had the opportunity to read the Bible for themselves. Surely, an unparalleled transformation had taken place, and Christianity was at the heart of it.

Wherever Christianity goes, transformation follows. The result of the jump in literacy was the Reformation's quick advance through Europe. The printed page spread the teachings of the reformers with lightening speed. The scions of secular society have long forgotten that they would not have the ability to spread their ideas if it were not for the men of faith that advanced the printed word. The modern media, whether print, internet or TV, is simply an outgrowth of the methodologies of Reformation communication. The obvious difference is that the reformers were spreading *good* news; their information was transforming lives, not dredging for the most prurient stories they could find to titillate the masses.

It is curious that the very institutions that arose from the Reformation to educate minds in biblical principles were transformed into mediums of secular propaganda. What is now taught in public, or, more accurately, government schools, is a far cry from the purposes and objectives of the reformers. Essentially, public schooling was hijacked by an alien ideology—a pagan ideology.

The reformers never intended to set up schools that would undermine the biblical mandate of parents to diligently teach their children at home. Nor were these Reformation schools set up to brain wash or coerce individuals. Rather, if society was to function properly, biblical truth was to be the basis for life's roadmap. Without this truth, God's Law would be replaced by natural law. Sadly, this is exactly what happened over the years as the original concepts of public education became perverted.

Although the reformers felt that the Bible in and of itself was sufficient for all areas of life, as the years progressed, secular forces did not, and this was to impact the educational systems of both Europe and North America.

Nevertheless, the influence that these Reformation schools were having was profound, and was intellectually reshaping the Europe of the sixteenth century. The reformers emphasized universal education in hopes of bringing Europe to a point of one hundred percent literacy. Teaching in general came to be looked upon as a divine vocation, bringing people out of ignorance and poverty. If there were those with extraordinary intellectual abilities, they were to be given special education to refine and cultivate their gifts. Additionally, there was a major push to better educate the clergy. Semi-literate priests who had converted to Protestantism would now have to come up to the standard befitting of their office. After all, how could they possibly educate the masses if they themselves did not have a firm grasp of reading, and thus of better understanding the Bible?

The goal, however, was not just to reform the church, but to look after the betterment of society as a whole. Malancthon encapsulated this thought by insisting that the good brought about by literacy and learning was not just a religious matter, but also for "the interest of the public weal."

Calvin believed that it was the duty of every Christian to become as educated as possible for two reasons. First, so that the church would not become a "desert for our children"; that is, that biblical scholarship and clerical education would be of a high standard so that the church would prosper and not lose its focus. Second, education would be vital so that civil government could be administered by educated Christians, thus raising the moral and ethical bar of society as a whole.

In 1536, Calvin called for a public meeting in Geneva where the citizens of the city pledged to have their children educated at church sponsored schools.

John Knox created *The First Book of Discipline*, outlining a national system of education. Because of this reformer's insistence on education for all, Scotland was one of the first countries to climinate illiteracy, and went on to become perhaps the greatest missionary sending country.

The protestant clergy was quickly becoming the most educated group in Europe. Additionally, Europe was beginning to see an exponential rise in educated lay people who would also contribute to the public good. Even though our contemporary public education has fallen victim to secular humanism, the aura of respect for teachers remains until this day, an insignia of the Reformation ethos.

By the mid 1500's, European universities had been revitalized by the sweeping educational changes taking place. Revised curricula included extensive classes in rhetoric, classical languages, history and poetry. Once again, the universities assumed the headship of culture, where as before they were intellectually moribund.

One of the subjects that got a thorough going over was history. History was no longer seen as a study of secular society, but rather a tool in the hands of God, showing his sovereignty over the affairs of men. Luther himself tried to create a chart of secular and biblical history in an attempt to harmonize them. Sebastian Franck authored a comprehensive history of the world that was, at the time, revolutionary, in that it placed God and redemption at the center of all history. He did, however, go to excesses in his spiritualism, speaking often of a mystical church that would arise out of Protestantism, superior to the contemporary sects of the day.

Let us pause for a moment and consider the pagan mindset on the issue of education. First, in the ancient world any real education was experienced only by the ruling classes. We often associate Greece as the center of culture and learning in the ancient world, and this reputation is well supported. However, the ancient city states of Greece were more interested in producing brutal warriors than great intellectuals.

For example, Sparta was known, primarily, as a military state. They did have a mandatory education system, but in this system, the individual was told that the state, and the interests of the state, took precedent over human life; it was the preservation of the state that was all important. Healthy young men were immediately marked out for military training, many taken away from their parents at a young age. On the other hand, sickly children were brought up into the mountains to die.

Spartan society cared little for literacy or the arts. It was a society bent on building up the state, and on military conquest. The goal was to breed warriors capable of brutal acts. Appeasing the gods was done for no other reason than to ensure victory on the battlefield. A master race of warriors was their dream. Even Plato affirmed the Spartan use of eugenics to cull the population and allow only the fit to survive.[3]

The Third Reich with its desire to create an *Obermensch*, is simply an echo of this ancient, pagan mentality. Indeed, most Nazi ceremonies were rife with pagan symbolism, some taken directly from ancient occult practices. So the modern fascist is nothing more than a pagan practicing an old religion in a new way. The same could be said for communism, with its pantheon of leaders like Marx, Engels, Trotsky, Stalin and Mao, who are practically worshipped like gods, and whose written words are venerated as scripture.

Indeed, the Nazis marked out Jews in particular for extermination because the basis of all human ethics comes from the Bible, and if the Jews in the Old Testament were entrusted with the oracles of God, then they were in competition with the god-man that the Nazis sought to create. Thus in order for the Nazi pagan mentality to rule, the Jews had to be eliminated.[4]

While it is often thought that the Nazis were Christians gone amok, nothing could be further from the truth; they were pagans practicing a form of pagan worship. Just about every form of paganism has some form of death cult. It usually centers on the sacrifice of a victim, either from within the cult, or an enemy of the cult. Clearly, communism and Nazism killed both their own members and their enemies. In paganism's killing of a victim, the hope is to appease their particular god—or Satan—and in doing so gain some kind of blessing, power or advantage over their adversaries.

It is not difficult to see that the aforementioned is nothing more than a mockery of the vicarious death of Christ. The pagan, in his various rituals, chants and incantations, is bringing damnation upon himself and those assenting to the acts performed.

The literacy that the Reformation spawned was a direct attack on the pagan mentality, for even the lowly peasant who learned to read the Bible was freed from the grip of superstitions placed upon him by either the Roman Catholic institution, or the pagan culture at large. To read is to be free. This was a most holy goal for the Reformers: to free the minds of Europeans and others by teaching them to read the biblical texts for themselves.

The continuing surge of educated gentry was also a major factor in the advance of culture in Europe. England, although in much religious turmoil in the sixteenth century, was beginning to feel the warming effects of the Reformation. New and improved schools resulting from the influence of Reformation thinkers and educators, brought higher education to a broader range of the populous. This burst of learning set the stage for writers and thinkers like Francis Bacon, Sir Philip Sidney, Edmund Spenser and Shakespeare.

We would be amiss not to mention the effects of the Reformation on science, also. An interesting parallel exists, for example, between Luther and Copernicus. Luther sought to make Christianity "Son-centered," while Copernicus put forth the idea—correctly—that the sun was at the center of our solar system, and that the earth and other planets revolved around it.

Aside from this seeming coincidence, Luther taught that the scholastics and humanists of his day did not fully appreciate nature. He argued that the Creation narrative and the Incarnation call for a closer examination and appreciation of the natural, material world.[5] Luther put scientific inquiry in a better light as he insisted that science and the Bible were in harmony, not at war with each other. The fact that the universe was created *ex nihilo* by God, Luther felt, should be cause for scientific celebration as it was a direct manifestation of the Creator. If so, then to discover more about the created order was to discover more about God.

This thinking essentially unchained many who were reticent to enter the scientific realm because of religious reservations, thinking that the scientific method would shake their faith. For most, the contrary was true. As they delved into their scientific studies, their faith was strengthened, and their zeal for discovery was elevated.

The influence of the Reformation made Luther's time period receptive to scientific investigation. Name a new invention, and the Germans were most likely interested in it, or were busy perfecting it. Whether it was in the area of the printing press, the clock, metallurgy or medicine, the Germans were a busy people in their pursuit of a better quality of life. Luther was quick to attack superstitions, and even quicker to affirm new scientific discoveries.

As we have mentioned before, the idea that Christianity supplants one myth for another, simply does not hold. The reformers were not fearful of scientific discovery as something that would weaken the faith of the masses, but rather saw it as a tool in the hands of the believer to demonstrate the creative nature of God, and the profundity of His universe.

On and on rolled the scientific inquiries of this time. Conrad Gesner, a Swiss biologist devised a new system for cataloging flora and fauna. Leonard Fuchs, a German, produced a glossary of botanical terms. The Italian Niccolo Tartaglia was the first to solve the cubic equation and to develop the use of coefficients.[6] Intellectual curiosity was being fueled by the idea that knowing more science was a religious duty.

The world owes much to the reformers in the area of education, and since the reformers were simply echoing the will of their Creator, the world needs to put intellectual and scientific progress squarely on the shoulders where it belongs: the Christian culture.

---

1   Lewis W. Spitz, *The Protestant Reformation: 1517-1520* (New York: Harper & Row, 1985), pp. 89ff

2   Ibid., p.94

3   Karl R. Popper, *The Open Society and Its Enemies, Vol. I, The Spell of Plato* (London: Routledge & Kegan Paul, 1969), p.7

4   Scott Lively, Kevin E. Abrams, *The Pink Swastika* (Keizer, Oregon: Founders Publishing, 1995), preface, viii

5   *The Protestant Reformation*, p.380

6   op. cit., pp. 381-383

NINE
The Puritans Make Their Mark

SOMEONE ONCE SAID that the Puritan ethic could be summed up by the fear that somewhere, somehow, there might be people having a good time. But the stereotypes that many hold regarding these often mocked believers belie the legacy that they have left us, to which we should pay tribute.

There is an amicable debate among scholars as to what constitutes the Puritan era. We would be safe to say, however, that it spans approximately from the late sixteenth century to the early part of the eighteenth century. The Puritans were called such because they wanted to "purify" the Church of England. As Reformation changes swept across Europe, it seemed that the weakest link in the chain was England. The Puritans sought to bring the national church into total conformity with the Word of God, but they were met with much opposition and persecution. Queen Elizabeth did all she could to block many of the reforms they sought. By the time Charles I came to the throne, many saw the whole situation as hopeless and left for the New World.

Our focus here is not an examination of Puritan history, but rather the Puritan ideal. That is, what made the Puritans so special? Why were they so persecuted, and why did they have such an impact on the New World?

The Puritans were viewed by many as radical reformers. They had a comprehensive view of the Christian life. While many see them as tight lipped censors, the reality is that the Puritans sought balance in the Christian life. That balance extended from the church to civil government. The Puritans were not mere observers or hermits. Rather, they sought to bring the biblical principles they saw in scripture to bear upon all aspects of human life.

In their view, all creation was the Lord's, and it was the duty of Christians to be sure that no area of their lives was out of concord with the Creator's intentions. This would include, as we discussed in our last chapter, a desire for scientific discovery and new inventions, although, to be sure, these were not their primary emphases.

If we were to pinpoint the heart of Puritan genius, it would be their view of man. The Puritans were Calvinists, and held to the total depravity of man. Men and women are not basically good; they are fallen and need to depend on God absolutely for their redemption. Man cannot earn any merit in the eyes of God apart from Christ. While they insisted on good works both among the brethren and in the community, those good works accounted for nothing toward their salvation. Good works were viewed as the fruit of salvation, not the cause.

The work ethic of western culture that so many admire can be traced, if not directly, then indirectly, to the Puritans. Christians were to be upright in all their labors. A workman was, in reality, employed by God, and must work as if his very life depended on it. So armed with this idea, a man could transform his community, indeed, the world, for Christ. The community of man was their concern. All people needed to heed the call of Christ and to live internally and externally as Christ would have them live.

To change the world, one must have a hopeful view of the future. The Puritans had that—and then some. Their view of the future was marked by a very positive eschatology. They did not believe that the world would disintegrate into chaos just prior to the return of Christ. No, rather, the gospel would be victorious—the gates of hell would *not* prevail against Christ's church: Every pagan idea, every concept that did not square with the New Testament, every religion that mocked the deity of Christ, must and would be defeated. In the end, the standard of Christ and His Gospel would be planted on the foundations of the earth for all to see. If not, then Christ's redemptive work and God's will could be thwarted, a concept absolutely alien to the Puritan mind.

The Puritans also placed a strong emphasis on spiritual revival. They not only wanted to convert the heathen, they also wanted to revive a slumbering church, get it up on its feet, and off to work in the harvest fields of the world. Revival was another tool in the workshop of Puritans thinkers, for it gave the church a direction; a way to turn "sightseeing" Christians into actual participants, both in the work of the church and in their civic duties.

When the Puritans came to America to escape religious persecution in their homeland, their stated goal was to establish a "city on a hill"; a society that would be a great example to the world, and, in particular, to England, where they hoped to some day return. Their hope was that their new communities would be exemplary in behavior, and thus prompt the Church of England to repent. They also believed that the Reformation was becoming weak in Europe due to the great sin of the people there, who refused to fully embrace the purity that Christ intended for His church.

Conversion of the heathen was of primary importance to them, and they believed that conversion came in particular stages: Introspection, self-condemnation; then revived hope in God—and finally, the realization of grace.

Conversion for the Puritan was the first essential needed for civic life. No one could hold an office in the local government if they were not proved to be a true and practicing Christian. Those who held civic offices were to exude Christian values and judgment. The concept of "separation of church and state" was alien to the Puritans, for all of life was sacred, and must be governed as such under the auspices of biblical principles. Therefore, how could an unredeemed man or woman govern properly since they did not understand the very principles that governed life itself?

Public and private affairs were to have their foundation in the Bible. To the secular observer, this is a prescription for trouble, since to not conform to the "norm" would make one suspect, and might even incur the wrath of officials. But to say that there was no variation in Puritan life would be a mistake. Certainly, there were differences of opinion in all spheres, but the idea was that there would be a general agreement on theological issues. This would translate into correct moral thinking, and result in a unified society largely free from crime, sexual deviance and graft. Society was to be united under God, according to His Word, and His will.

To our twenty first century ears, this is all a bit odd. What about free speech? What about expressing yourself? What about "live and let live"?

We must remember that to the Puritan, the aforementioned would strike *them* as odd. The idea of a "free" society was not everyone doing whatever they pleased, but rather, *what pleased God.* They took the admonition in 2 Corinthians 6:17 to heart: "Come out from their midst and be separate" (NASB). Like all major movements, Puritanism had its failings. However, the ideals it stood for formed the pillars upon which truly free societies stand.

We need not look far to see how Puritanism was the polar opposite of paganism. Followers of the "ancient religion," that is, paganism in its more obvious forms (e.g., witchcraft, satanism, and goddess worship, etc.), have a credo: "Do what thou will shall be the whole of the law!" This antinomianism, or lawlessness, is at the heart of paganism, whether it actually takes the form of a religion that worships a deity, or simply manifests itself as rebellion against all authority. Many would argue that the Puritans were "law abiders" in the strictest sense, and that this tendency pushed them over the top into stifling cruelty. The Puritans were not perfect, and we should remember that they would be the first ones to say so. They saw themselves as sinners just like everyone else, but they attempted to lead a life "by the book" instead of "by the flesh." Their "ordered" life is a reflection of the Creator's intention, for He created all things *ex nihilo*, i.e., "from nothing," and He expects men and women created in His image to also be "creators" via hard work and innovation.

One of the great plagues of the modern world is lack of proper time management. This is usually the case because modern men and women spend their time in pursuit of things that do not edify the soul. The T.V., radio or computer has now taken the place of the quiet and reflective time our forefathers spent reading and considering their place in the universe and their relationship with God. When you consider the great body of written work that the Puritans have left us, you realize that these were a people serious about the Christian life; no stone was left unturned in their relentless war against sin.

Western countries today have tasted the rotten fruit of lawlessness and social rebellion that was planted in the 1960's. To everyone that would upbraid the Puritans for their seemingly "over the top and uptight" attitude toward personal and social morals, we should be quick to ask, "What kind of society would you choose to live in? One that is ordered, law abiding and prosperous, or one that is anarchic, dangerous and lost in economic mire?"

The road to pagan social disorder begins when the foundations of biblical teaching are attacked. The Puritans, frail and human as they were, put the bar of social and religious order way up; not unreachable, but far enough up to keep society from falling into the vortex of spiritual confusion. Unfortunately, pagan philosophy under the guise of rational and scientific thought would soon mount an assault on all that is holy.

TEN
The Worldly Philosophers Mount an Assault

THE STEREOTYPICAL VIEW OF PAGANISM as those who bow down to a wood or stone god or who dance around a fire while praising mother earth belies a more sinister form of worship: vain philosophy.

The human mind apart from the regenerative power of the Holy Spirit is a deep pit waiting to engulf its next victim. As John Calvin once remarked, our hearts are "idol factories," and our carnal minds run to the alleged "truths" of this world in their desire for more knowledge.

The eighteenth century brought with it a strong anti-Christian furor, fueled by philosophic intellectual inquiry. We may well ask how this came about as the two preceding centuries were filled with great religious fervor and monumental spiritual victories. To answer this question we would do well to note that along with the great spiritual victories of the sixteenth and seventeenth centuries came much conflict also. The in-fighting among many of the reformers spilled into the political realm, shaking, at times, the entire social landscape. If we take England as an example, we simply have to look at the religious perturbations during the reigns of Henry VIII, Edward VI, Mary and Elizabeth. Even the most zealous reformer would have to admit that much upheaval was created even as the chains of Catholicism were dissolving.

All of this provided fertile ground for the anti-Christian skeptic. When this is combined with the great scientific advancements sweeping across Europe at the same time, it is easy to see that the bent of philosophy was going to take on a more empiricist view.

Indeed, it did, practically declaring war on the faith—and the people who professed faith.

This period, called the "The Enlightenment" or "The Age of Reason" was anything but. Deism was already taking a strong hold among the *intelligentsia*, so it was a short step to official "Rationalism."

The basic premise of this period was that only things that are "rational" could be trusted as being "real," or worthy of truth. Thus, anything related to faith, God and religion, was held as suspect at best, and chicanery at worst. The core of this philosophic understanding had to do with the senses. John Locke, perhaps the greatest proponent of the empirical method, and an admitted nominal Christian, stated that all we know; colors, textures, words and so forth, are assimilated by our senses. This is how we understand our world. Therefore, we do not understand our world by religious notions of some other world "out there," or suprasensational "feelings." The human being is simply a *tabla rasa*, a "blank slate" upon which the external world imprints impressions; nothing more, nothing less. Our conscience is the sum total of these things. So, when we react a certain way or say that we perceive something in a certain way, what we are saying is, "I am reacting according to the sum of the knowledge and experience I have gained from the senses."

Of course, much of what is being said is true; we get our impressions of the physical universe from our senses. From this there is agreement as to what constitutes, for example, "red" or that sandpaper is rough. However, the empiricists were wary of any talk of the supernatural. After all, was not much blood shed in the name of religion? Moreover, is not religion the road block to all human progress? If so, to eliminate religion, or at least, dependence on the supernatural, would free man. This freedom would allow him to truly enjoy life apart from the shackles of religious zealots. Man could now seek new scientific discoveries without the church breathing down his neck, censoring his works, and thus impeding human progress.

Perhaps the man most noted for his attack on religion, Christianity in particular, was the Frenchman, Voltaire. He questioned the logic of Christianity, and even its morality: Could a brutally crucified man be at the core of a loving religion? Voltaire, indeed, was the enemy of the faith, and is probably the father of social rebellion, in that all morality was up for grabs to him. He called Christianity *L'Infame*, and showed complete contempt for the doctrine of the atonement.

If we ask how far to the left Europe had come since the formative days of the Reformation, consider this: In 1778, after living in Germany and Switzerland for many years, Voltaire returned to Paris and was received with great zeal and accolades. Every artisan and intellectual wanted to meet the great Voltaire, the man who had single-handedly cut the legs out from under religion. Clearly, Europe had become engulfed in a sea of humanism.

Whether one was a rationalist, who believed that we can know things and gain knowledge intuitively, or an empiricist who relied solely on the senses and that which could be overtly proved, the focus was nevertheless away from the Bible and the idea of the supernatural.

Christians had always contended that God was the cause of all things. Thomas Aquinas, the great twelfth century theologian, called God the "Primary Cause." Aquinas reasoned that if one looks at all things and causes and keeps going back and back in time, the only thing left would be God; and thus He is the cause of all things. This conclusion is based on logic and the belief in a divine being that can create *ex nihilo*.

In contrast, by the middle of the eighteenth century, David Hume was challenging this type of thinking, if not trying to dismantle it. We can never know anything, he claimed, *a prior;* i.e., by knowing it outside of experience. Cause and effect are eternally linked to *experience*. At first blush, one may claim that there is nothing wrong with this proposition. However, to statements like, "I have experienced God" or perhaps, "I have *experienced* God's forgiveness," Hume would reply, "How have you experienced God like one would experience rain or a hammer hitting your thumb?" That is, what is the empirical data you can present? To which you might rejoin, "I can't actually prove it, I know it by the spirit intuitively."

Hume's reply to all this would be: "Nonsense! You can never know anything apart from true experience. Reason and intuition have nothing to do with it!"

To the person of faith, the problem here is obvious: *One can never have experience apart from experience.* Stated another way, if the experience comes from your "mind" rather than something that is externally observable, it is not true experience, and thus it is *not* knowledge. According to Hume, we can never, therefore, make statements like, "I'm forgiven by God," or "I feel the joy of the Lord," or anything of the sort, for how can we objectively prove that?

Even imagination or flights of fancy have their genesis in the empirical experience. They are simply random pieces of that which we already have true knowledge of, not creations in and of themselves.

Hume attempted to place everything within the boundaries of "quantity and number"; that is, objective "science" as it was. Everything else for him was pure "sophistry and illusion." The existence of any being can only be proven by arguments from its cause or effect. These arguments must be based squarely on experience.

In effect, any "spiritual" insights we have gained or claim to have are not that at all, but are the ruminations of our temporal experience. They may very well be real to us, but they have no basis in real experience *per se*.

Following on the heels of Hume was Immanuel Kant, one of the most influential philosophers of all time—and, perhaps, the most complex. For Kant and Hume, we cannot divorce ourselves from experience in our description of the empirical world. However, Kant differed from Hume in that he believed that the mind had an innate *a priori* sense of things. That is, the mind was prepared to receive and properly process knowledge as it experienced things in the material world. Simply put, the mind had all the *preconditions*, if you will, necessary to make sense of things.

But the knowledge that we gain is synthetic; it must be "put together" by experience and all preconditions. Kant outlined this line of thinking in his copious and monumental work *Critique of Pure*

Reason (1781). This work was followed by a more popular treatment of the subject in *Prolegomena* (1783).

Kant believed that there existed a metaphysical concept, but not the traditional one. Rather, one that is analytical in nature, which has as its base the experiential world.

In his 1784 essay, "An Answer to the Question: What is Enlightenment?," the philosopher first defined "enlightenment" as "man's emergence from his self-imposed immaturity." He stated that man has relied too much on others outside himself to determine the nature of reality: "If I have a book to serve as my understanding, a pastor to serve as my conscience...I need not exert myself at all." Of course, this statement almost assumes that one is not thinking and developing conclusions on one's own, and simply taking what one is hearing or reading as a statement of fact.

You may very well ask, "I understand that this type of philosophy would impact biblical faith, but how can it be termed 'paganism' in its truest sense?"

Of course, this is a very good question, but one that can be dutifully answered. We must first remember that paganism need not be simply, as we have stated, men and women literally bowing down to a wood or stone statue. Any system that exalts itself above biblical precedent is "pagan" by its very nature. In the example of Kant that we have just outlined, intuitive *fideism* (i.e., the belief that affirms that the fundamental act of human knowledge consists in an act of faith, from *fide*, Latin for "faith"), is totally eliminated. Thus, if we follow Kant's thinking to its ultimate conclusion, we can never know God, for example, unless we actually see and experience Him directly in the material world. Now, if Kant were alive today, he probably would debate this as an oversimplification. Nevertheless, this is the only conclusion we can draw from his systematized concepts.

Taking this discussion for a moment into the realm of Christian apologetics, we see how Kant's reasoning cuts at the very root of the testimony of the spirit, in particular, the Holy Spirit, in the life of the believer.

When one affirms the existence of God, there are usually two main arguments that are put forward as proof. One is the *teleological* argument; the other is the view of *fideism*, which we have outlined above. The teleological argument is the argument from design. That is, if we look at the universe and biological life, we see order and complexity, which in turn leads us to conclude that a Divine Creator made everything we see. The fideist argument says that no matter how much "proof" you present, the existence of God is found in the testimony of the Spirit that converts the soul to believe in Jesus Christ as the only begotten Son of God. Hence, the centrality of this belief is faith, *not* empirical data.

Clearly, Kant's reasoning negates the testimony of the Spirit, especially in the realm of conversion. Moreover, the testimony of God to men came via the Holy Spirit of God. Consider Mark 12:36:

> *David himself, in the Holy Spirit, declared,*
> *"'The Lord said to my Lord,*
> *Sit at my right hand,*
> *until I put your enemies under your feet.'"*

In the above passage, David was "in the Holy Spirit"; that is, filled and directed by the Holy Spirit. In the present New Testament age, now that the canon is closed, people no longer receive direct revelations from God, but we see how God did speak at one time via the prophets by way of the Holy Spirit.

The Enlightenment philosophers, in their attempt to "free man," instead enslaved him to his own sophistry. Man apart from the direct intervention of God is a wondering cloud, blown about by the winds of his own making.

In order to find his way out of the labyrinth of this world, man needs a Savior, One who created a culture of life in the Spirit.

ELEVEN
The Evangelical Spirit of Reform

WHILE THE ENLIGHTENMENT PHILOSOPHERS sought change in the way men thought, and thus the social order, it was really evangelicals who were changing the world. Men and women who had truly trusted Christ as Savior, and who took the message of the Bible seriously, were in the vanguard of compassionate change.

The rapid industrialization of the western world, England in particular, fueled the increase of missionary and progressive church activity. The nineteenth century saw a virtual explosion of Christian societies that were busy in both evangelical activity and social reform.

England had seen the gross excesses that the French revolution brought about, and it was more than wary about humanistic philosophies guiding the future of the country. After all, the French revolution was ignited by the Enlightenment, and while it did bring about a republic, it also brought much bloodshed and antipathy toward Christianity.

What was really revolutionary was the freedom that many evangelicals felt to step outside of the mainline churches to form organizations for *ad hoc* purposes. This allowed more and more missionaries to be sent all over the world with fewer encumbrances.

Men like John Wesley and George Whitfield had already set a torrid pace for evangelizing the lost, in addition to reviving a tepid body of believers. What the Enlightenment could never do, the new evangelical spirit was accomplishing: personal and social change. Witness organizations like The Society for Bettering the Conditions of the Poor (circa 1796). This organization built shelters for the homeless, protected abused wives and children, fed the hungry, and lobbied for better working conditions in the burgeoning factories. Evangelicals were at the forefront of reaching out to the poor, the widows, and the orphans.

Perhaps even more significant was the evangelical attack on the institution of slavery. Far from being blasé or even supporting this evil—of which Christians have always been accused—evangelicals led the way for terminating this most hideous practice.

By the mid-eighteenth century, slavery was considered absolutely necessary to the economic health of the British Empire. Consider that by 1770 more than half of the slaves coming out of West Africa were owned and transported by English merchants. However, at the same time, organized groups of evangelicals were making passionate appeals to both Parliament and the British people. Again and again they hammered away at the British conscience. How, they asked, could a Christian nation tolerate the selling of human beings like chattel? How could Englishmen sleep at night knowing that their country sponsored such cruelty?

To drive home their point, evangelical abolitionists, like their Reformation brothers and sisters before them, made great use of the written word. Tracts, booklets and full-blown tomes were the order of the day—and they were eagerly consumed by an interested public.

It was the evangelical spirit of Christian persistence and compassion that on February 23, 1807, lead Parliament to finally end the horror of trafficking in human lives. English ships would no longer fill their holds with men and women in chains. Slaves already under the lash were not free, but it was a monumental step forward.

Once again, we see in the abolitionist movement the compassion and progressive nature of Christianity. The lame charges of an atavistic, one-dimensional religion out of step with the modern world, is simply false. Other so-called "progressive" movements, in particular global communism, that had its beginnings in the mid 1840's, did virtually nothing for those in chains, except to deride capitalism and the free market system for creating such an evil. Yet, over the next one hundred plus years, communism would kill millions; accrue absolute power in the countries ruled by it via an overly centralized government—to say nothing of destroying the faith of many.

Because of the great successes of the evangelical movement in Britain, prominent members of the Church of England sought to erect barriers by claiming what it felt was its rightful place: the *one* and *only* church of the English people. This lead to a series of writings being issued affirming the absolute authority of the church, that the Anglican priests were successors of the apostles; and that the sacraments had actual soul-saving powers.

Most of all, these writings leveled a vicious attack on anything "Protestant," saying that "Protestantism" and schism and confusion went hand in hand. The Church of England, they said, must stand as a unified whole, or drown in a sea of spiritual anarchy.

Nevertheless, this attack on non-Anglican Protestants failed to halt the juggernaut of evangelical social movements in England, as well as in Europe in general. Evangelicals were in the vanguard of the struggle to help the "have nots" and the oppressed. Even today in Third World countries, Christian organizations are the ones building hospitals, clinics and shelters for the poor, and most of all, meeting their spiritual needs.

The stark reality is that humanism, whether in the guise of "progressive movements" or actual pagan religious beliefs, has utterly failed to address the deepest needs of the human heart. Conversely, where the banner of Christianity is held high, the light of hope shines the brightest.

TWELVE
A Country of Destiny

THE FORMATION OF A GROUP of rag-tag colonies into the most powerful country the world has ever seen is a story of almost mythic proportions. The American saga is unique to world history, and so we need to look briefly at some salient points regarding America, religion, paganism and the forging of a nation.

The American nation has had, perhaps, the greatest effect on world Christianity. It is even more interesting to study the initial foundations of the country as they give us insights into its structural guidelines that were firmly based on the Bible.

Many initially came to the North American continent to escape religious persecution. They not only brought with them their faith, but incredible intellectual prowess. It is at this point that we must step back and make some clarifications. We are not going to attempt to say that America was founded in an era of complete Christian orthodoxy, for the landscape of American religion during the formation of the republic was a very complex one.

Indeed, the purity of religion that the Puritans sought to bring to fruition in America was quickly diminished by the residue of Enlightenment thought that filtered into the colonies. Emigration brought many from Europe who imbibed at the well of skepticism. Deism had an extremely strong hold on many, despite the heroics of faithful evangelists. Therefore, any study of the formation of the American nation must take this into consideration.

It is true that a number of the Founding Fathers of America were deists. Yet, this fact should not obscure the many more that were orthodox in their theology, and wanted to be sure that the country followed the guiding principles of Scripture at its onset. Herein, however, is the paradox: *both deist and Christian alike felt that the foundational teaching of the New Testament, and the law paradigm outlined by the Old Testament, needed to be incorporated into the documents of confederation.*

It is therefore completely legitimate to say that the Christian religion was at the center of the founding of the country. Moreover, it is astounding that these two groups of men came together under the gravity of biblical principles.

At this point, you may protest, "But what is the difference between a well-educated colonist who is a deist and does not believe in the deity of Jesus Christ, and a pagan bowing down to a statue in some savage land? Do not both share the same fate?"

This is an excellent question and certainly one that Christians need to grapple with. What this question does, oddly enough, is show the power of the Christian message and the fact that if one indeed wants to start a country that will be in order and prosperous, one could not find better guidelines than those found in the Christian Scriptures. We first off do not want to run away from the question. Yes, pagan and deist share the same fate—as does anyone who denies the deity of Christ and His vicarious, atoning death on the cross: hell. The Bible is very clear on this. John 3:18 states, "He who believes in Him is not condemned; but he who does not believe is condemned already because he has not believed in the name of the only begotten son of God." Because deists simply refuse to believe that God intervened directly in the affairs of men through Jesus Christ, the only begotten Son of God, they are condemned along with the pagan who is bowing down to his wood statue.

We would point out, however, that the deists in the American colonies were surrounded by a Christian culture. This caused them to grapple—however they may have objected—with those issues that were particularly Christian. That is, they were denying the deity of Christ, but maintaining the moral standard of the New Testament. Pagans, per se, care nothing of a moral standard, except, perhaps, if Mother Earth is harmed in some way or their mode of worship is threatened.

The fact is that the Founding Fathers, regardless whether they were Christians or deists, believed that the main purpose of government was to restrain evil. This is indeed a biblical concept. Man is a fallen creature, he needs to be redeemed—and while he is on this earth there must be restraints. The institution of government was put here by God to keep man under control; government stands in the place of God in the social realm:

> *Romans 13:1-2 Let every soul be subject to the governing authorities. For there is no authority except from God, and the authorities that exist are appointed by God. Therefore, whoever resists the authority resists the ordinance of God, and those who resist will bring judgment on themselves.*

Paganism is not interested in social restraint. Instead, by openness to social aberration, it brings on extreme forms of hedonism. We therefore see that Christianity exerts an influence on society, even if certain individuals governing that society are not what we would call "believing Christians." Moreover, the Founding Fathers paved the way for the free exercise of religion. It just so happens that the majority of the people in the colonies *were* Christians.

The "Establishment Clause" of the Constitution was to prevent a state church from arising—as in the case of England—*not* to prevent the free exercise of religion, or to stifle the mention of religious beliefs in the public forum, including public (or government) schools.

As to the underlying question as to whether or not the United States was founded on the Christian faith, we point to some of the founding documents of the settlers and colonies of the early seventeenth century.

As early as 1606, the charter for the Virginia Colony read:

> *"To the glory of His divine majesty, in propagating the Chris-*

tian religion to those who as yet live in ignorance of the true knowledge and worship of God."

The Mayflower Compact of 1620 says this:

"For the glory of God and the advancement of the Christian faith [we] combine ourselves together into a civil body politic."

The Fundamental Orders of Connecticut (1639) were created to:

"...maintain and preserve the liberty and purity of the Gospel of our Lord Jesus Christ..."

Clearly, it was the spirit of the Gospel that compelled these men and women to form a new nation. While not all was orthodox in their theology, the *principles* of the faith were carried forth and reflected in the new republic's government structure. Certainly there was the ebb and flow of religious zeal. However, The Great Awakening of the 1700's energized a dormant evangelicalism in the colonies, and gave impetus to sending missionaries to the outermost reaches of the world. The effects of the Great Awakening extended far into the nineteenth century and permanently shaped the moral outlook of America.

While deism was held by many of the Founding Fathers, it was always a minority philosophy in the quilt work of America. Held by many of the educated upper classes, deism still could not stop the spread of the Gospel among the colonists and their children—or convince them that their faith was simplistic and in vain.

It might be said that deism was a form of paganism dressed in its Sunday best. Deism claimed such intellectual giants as Thomas Jefferson and Thomas Paine, although Paine is sometimes inaccurately classified as a "Founding Father." It can also be said that this philosophy had an effect years later on biblical scholarship, particularly in the so-called "higher" school of biblical criticism.

At first, this connection may not seem apparent, and one may be inclined to say that this is an "apples and oranges" idea. The truth, however, is that where the authority of Scripture is diminished, liberal theology follows. Deism taught that God did exist, but that He was a passive god who wound the universe up like a giant clock, set it in motion—and now sits back as history unfolds, uninterested in the affairs of men.

Likewise, the goal of paganism is one that is either passive, like the god of deism, or wildly aggressive in its attempt to shake the foundations of a Christianized society. Therefore, the questioning of scriptural authority or its historicity (as with the "higher criticism") brings the pagan mindset to the fore. Deism did not deny God; it sought to create a god that would be more palatable to the minds of mere humans. That, in fact, is what liberal theology does—and *that* is the essence of paganism: creating a god that is more like men and women, imperfect and frail.

In recent years, "open theism" has taken this one step further, saying that God cannot know the future, and suffers along with mankind.

American evangelicals have remained resilient, though, even when coming face to face with these heresies. No other country's Christian population has given more money, time, and effort to relief causes. Even America's secular philanthropists are such because of the influence of the Gospel on this good, yet still very sinful, nation.

The ultimate battlefield for the minds and hearts of the American people—indeed, all people of good conscience--will not be in the streets or on the picket lines though, but in the classrooms of government schools. It is therefore necessary to turn once again to the idea of education and its interaction with Christianity.

We will do so in the next chapter.

THIRTEEN
The Rise and Fall of Government Schooling

WE MENTIONED EARLIER that the reformers created public education to teach the illiterate to read. This served two purposes: it gave the individual in question a better temporal life; now they could read and perhaps improve their lot, and, secondly, and most importantly, they could be instructed in the Scriptures and gain insight into eternal life.

The second major point we need to remind ourselves of is that the Establishment Clause was created to prevent a state church from arising to the exclusion of others. It was not created to squelch the free exercise of religion, or to curtail the public proclamation of the gospel.

The early settlers of the North American continent saw the church and the state as equal partners. If people wanted to express their faith in different ways, fine. But they also felt that civil law was subservient to biblical law, and any government that wanted to stick around had better use the Bible as its guiding rule book.

It is interesting to note that James Madison, one of the primary architects of the Constitution, fully understood that the concept for public education started in the reformation. He knew that public schooling was a way to prepare men and women for a life that was glorifying to God. Therefore, public education had its origin in religious consciousness, Christian consciousness in particular. In this instance, we use the term "public education" in its original sense: schools set up by the public, for the public, for the benefit of the public. What is now called public schooling is not even a shadow of what it was originally meant to be.

The reformers certainly knew that if people were to truly worship God in spirit and in truth, they must know that salvation was by grace alone. In order to break the yoke that had been placed on the minds of the people by the Roman church, this fact had to be communicated. Certainly "faith comes by hearing," and the masses were quick to absorb this life changing reality. The reformers, however, wanted more: they wanted people to read God's truth for themselves. Since the majority of sixteenth century European peasantry was illiterate, the simple solution was to teach them to read so that they and their progeny could enjoy God's truth.

We mentioned earlier that it was never the intention of the reformers to set up schools that would replace or undermine the biblical mandate of parents to diligently teach their children at home. Rather, if society was to function properly and efficiently, people needed to learn how to read. In particular, they needed to read the Bible. To not have the truth of the Bible would mean that natural law—the law solely from the mind of man—would prevail. Unfortunately, this is precisely what happened as the modern forms of paganism perverted the concept of public schooling: self-absorption, sexual confusion, anti-European historiography and the usurpation of parental control.

It is certainly true that in whatever country we find ourselves, that the government controlled schools there are a form of state mind control; their function is to inculcate the general values of the society at large and to ensure that anti-state ideas don't find their way into the culture. In essence, they are a form of state-sponsored propaganda. That is not to say that all of it is bad. There was a time, especially in American schools, where excellent values were inculcated into the minds of young people: selflessness, respect for authority, country and religious institutions and cleanliness.

As an historical aside, the great Patrick Henry opposed the Constitution as written on two grounds. First, because he felt it gave too much power to the central government and, second, *because it was not explicitly Christian.*

To fully understand the development of public schools, you must understand that, although overwhelmingly Christian, many of the colonists did not agree—or did not understand—the biblical mandate on education. This is quite apart from the reformers who felt that Scripture was the final word on all matters because it was God's blueprint for mankind. This would extend to civil matters as well as religious ones.

The average person living in the colonies at the time clung to the comforting words of Scripture and, indeed, it cannot be denied that this was the benchmark of the general culture. This is quite significant considering the assault that Christianity was taking from the various philosophical circles of the time. However, the public schools in the colonies were now being changed to the classical model of the Greco-Roman world, which was certainly a good model to follow, but the problem was the shift from "Scripture only" to "intellect only." Obviously, there was the weighty influence of the deists who were small in number, but most powerful in civic affairs.

This influence followed American schooling into the nineteenth century, although for many Americans even then, public schooling apart from the teachings of Jesus Christ was absolutely unthinkable. So much was this fact a part of American culture, that the conservative theologian A.A. Hodge said, prophetically, that a centralized state-sponsored education "separated from religion [i.e., Christianity] will prove most appalling" and that if it were allowed to continue unchecked would promote "atheism, nihilism...such as the world has never seen."

In Europe of the same period, it was clear to see that where the Church of England and Lutheranism prevailed, the state was subservient. Moreover, even a cursory look at early Puritan legislation shows that the state was simply an arm of the church. The Puritans, while being careful to obey their temporal leaders, nevertheless appealed to their conscience with intellectual aplomb.

However, by the middle of the nineteenth century came groups who opposed what they saw as stifling orthodoxy. In Massachusetts, for example, the Unitarians, being deft power brokers, grabbed control of public education in the state—and never let go. With the Unitarians firmly in control and secularizing legislation reaching a frenzied peak in 1850, religious education in public schools became suspect.

The tail end of the nineteenth century and the beginning of the twentieth also saw Protestant Christianity on the brink of disaster. Reeling from the impact of Darwinism, orthodox Christianity found itself in a battle to defend the biblical account of creation. The specter of modernism also began to arise in the churches. Modernism accepted Darwinism readily, and also challenged the supernaturalism of the Bible. Clearly, these things were simply an echo of deism.

The modernists were extremely zealous for their position, and this zeal began to spill into the courts. The modern pagan attack on the scriptures and the Christian faith had swung into full action. However, the reaction of the courts is most informative at this time. It did not appear that the courts were about to wave the white flag and immediately surrender to the modernist onslaught.

In the case of *Moore v. Monroe* (64 Iowa 367, 1884) where the plaintiff wanted to eliminate the Bible, the Lord's prayer and hymns from the classroom, the Supreme Court unanimously called constitutional the Iowa law that declared: "The Bible shall in no way be excluded from the classroom." This was a very significant ruling.

The reading of the King James Bible prior to the start of classes was challenged by the case of *Wilkerson v. City of Rome, GA* (152 GA 762, 1922). Once again, however, the court struck down the plaintiff's case saying that there was abundant evidence that the "founding pioneers" of America "did not have in mind to bring about a complete separation of church and state." In view of the many similar controversies brewing in our courts today, this is a stunning declaration! Of course, the question must be asked, "Why are these court cases not presented today when similar situations arise?"

It is clear that through the years the Supreme Court has been rather sympathetic to the idea of religion in the classroom. However, there was yet another thinly veiled pagan attempt to water down overt Christian teaching in the classroom.

We refer specifically to the influence of secular educational philosophers, whose influence cannot be denied. Probably the most influential was John Dewey, who plunged America head-long into the arms of humanistic curricula by declaring that all life, including education, was shaped solely by material forces.

Influenced heavily by Darwinist thinking, Dewey formulated a basic theory of education that conveniently left God out of the equation. For Dewey, education was not a part of life—it *was* life. The dark side of this theory soon became apparent, as many children who were exposed to this rationale soon left the value system of their parents. Essentially, Dewey taught that one's cultural heritage had to be totally reformulated.

Thus, in their rush to extract religion from the classroom, the modern crop of philosophers created a new religion unto itself: secular humanism. While this term has almost become a cliché, and has even been mocked by those who subscribe to it, this philosophy is a *legally recognized reality*. The famous footnote from the case of *Torcaso v. Watkins* (367 U.S. Report p.465, footnote 11), states that there are religions that do not necessarily teach a belief in God, such as "Buddhism, Taoism…and secular humanism…"

This religious definition, when compared to what is actually happening in the schools, is quite incriminating. Secular humanism is, in fact, being taught in the public schools. This philosophy is being introduced via so-called "change agents"; that is, educators whose job it is to enter the public school system and recommend "changes." This, of course, begs the question: change to what?

The Elementary and Secondary School Act [1965] allowed the federal government to promote federally developed curricula in the public schools. Moreover, federal agencies like the National Endowment for the Humanities and the National Science Foundation are the real source of funding for many local public schools.

As with most governmental programs, a bureaucracy was formed to promote the program itself. The National Diffusion Network is a federally controlled agency whose task it is to promote "exemplary" programs across state lines. With federal funding, federal programs and federal manipulation, Big Brother education cannot be far behind.

A close inspection of the programs that are promoted by this agency only leads to the conclusion that "values clarification" equates to challenging—and then dismantling—every traditional religious belief. More than this, traditional beliefs are not just being challenged and dismantled, they are being replaced. This replacement comes in the form of either New Age "touchy-feely" flotsam, or "diversity," which usually translates into some kind of anti-European brainwashing. Dare we forget acceptance of "alternative lifestyles," read: homosexuality.

So what are we to make of all this? It would certainly seem that a precedent has been set from which there is no return. How can we say that Christianity has had any victory in this situation?

The answer is simply that when confronted by what seems to be a wall much too high to scale, the Christian faith bounds over it, fueled by the opposition's vigor. This has been the case with the ever expanding homeschool movement. Christians of all stripes have decided that the biblical mandate is for real, that the public schools have an agenda hostile to the faith; and that from a spiritual and academic standpoint, homeschooling is the right option.

Has homeschooling really caught on? Consider that in 1994 there were approximately 360,000 children between the ages of six and seventeen being homeschooled in the United States. A mere five years later in 1999, that figure had grown to 790,000.[1] By 2005 this ballooned to an estimated 2,000,000. One of the positive outgrowths of this expansion from a Christian perspective is that there is at least one parent at home all the time, usually the mother, passing on traditional values to their child/children. This equates to a return of the nuclear family where Dad works and Mom stays home. If this trend continues, one would tend to think that, once again, Christian culture would emerge as the dominate bellwether for the future of the American home. Even by conservative estimates, this would not be a stretch.

Meanwhile, hundreds of Christian schools have opened over the last few years whose purpose is to return to traditional classroom education, with the world seen from a Christian perspective. Additionally, new colleges have been started whose focus is to propagate the Christian worldview, with hopes of also changing, for the good, law and politics. Patrick Henry College in Virginia is a good example of this. The school's website states their educational philosophy as follows:

> *Patrick Henry College believes that God is the source of all truth, be it spiritual, moral, philosophical, or scientific. For this reason, we seek to educate students in God's truth throughout the entire curriculum. Christian faith and genuine learning cannot be separated; neither is our Christian faith a mere addendum to the liberal learning process. Instead, our Christian faith precedes and informs all that we at Patrick Henry College study, teach, and learn.*

We have briefly outlined the revolution in the concept of "public" education brought on by pagan cultural philosophies, and the response from many in the Christian community. These philosophies are not a twenty-first century invention, but have their roots in Enlightenment thinking as manifested by the deists, many of whom are America's most revered historical figures. Christians, however, have not acquiesced to the prevailing secular culture, but have insisted on remaining true to their calling. The resourcefulness of Christians in the face of overwhelming opposition shows the resiliency of the Faith, and the faithfulness of the One who watches over them to provide for all their needs.

1 U.S. census report, working paper # 53, *Home Schooling in the United States: Trends and Characteristics*, 2001

FOURTEEN
The New Paganism

IT HAS BEEN SAID that we are now living in the "Post Christian Age." If one looks around at contemporary western culture, this seems to be the only conclusion that can be drawn. It appears that Christian culture and traditional values have been drummed out of existence. Western civilization seems to be awash in sexual promiscuity and greed.

But we have seen, as with the homeschooling movement, that Christian believers are still busy upholding biblical values, despite what the media or simple observation may tell us.

We would be blind, however, not to admit that western culture is no longer governed by the principles of the Bible. While we have shown that early twentieth century Supreme Court decisions stood firmly behind the family and the Bible, such is not the case anymore. The changing landscape of many western countries, in particular the influx of non-Christian immigrants, has diffused the Christian mindset. In their attempt to be fair—and politically correct—western cultures have blurred the lines between basic Christian social beliefs, and pagan religious influence. Now, if Christianity or Judaism is spoken of, Hinduism, Islam and Buddhism must also be mentioned.

Politicians are now fond of extolling the virtues of non-Christian religions, as well as one's choice not to believe in *any* god. Additionally, the church has not been innocent in the demise of its own influence. Church leaders have taken a back seat in the social realm, preferring to concentrate on church growth, a nascent Christian movement that has replaced doctrinal accuracy with "how-can-I-be-fulfilled" feel-goodism.

The baby boomers, who were dancing in the mud at Woodstock in 1969, are now the shapers of social and political policy. They may have replaced their tie-dyed shirts and love beads for pinstripes, but inside they are still counter culture. Once the church backed off as the major influence on morals and culture, the floodgates were opened to recreate a culture void of moral fences and caution signs; a society that does not acknowledge or fear God.

Every social evil that we find in society can be traced back to a lack of Godly fear. Americans, especially, are more apt to accept, rather than fear. Abortion has killed millions since the *Roe v. Wade* decision in 1973. Yet the killing of the unborn is labeled "choice" rather than murder. The baby in the womb is simply "POC" in medical terminology—"Product Of Conception."

A veil of euphemisms has fallen over everything that, at one time, would shock us. Thus, the diminishment of European ancestry is "diversity." Support for the homosexual agenda is called being "open and affirming." Not rebuking unacceptable social behavior is being "sensitive," and on it goes.

Once we understand that the pagan mindset is the self, for the self, and only for the self, the veil quickly falls. All the obfuscation in the world cannot hide the agenda behind the gentle words we use to make sociopathic behavior acceptable. Any attempt to repel the current mainstream is considered "backwards" or "insensitive."

One of the most effective ways that pagan culture uses to reformat society is the feminization of men. Over the last thirty years, the women's movement has been most aggressive in undermining the role of men. In fact, they have attacked both men *and* women who remain in traditional roles. To them, men are aggressive beasts who have physically, emotionally, and spiritually oppressed women for ages. Some would even go so far to say that a woman does not need a man, but through "sisterhood" can fulfill her every need. Of course the overtones in this statement point to homosexuality. With the advancement of medicine, particularly *in vitro* fertilization, and the acceptance of the homosexual lifestyle, the ultimate feminist dream has been realized: having children without the use of a man.

In Genesis 2:21-25, we read of the creation of woman. She was to be a "helper" to man, and to complement the created order. She was to be "bone of bone" and "flesh of flesh" for the man. Thus God created a specific role and order for men and women. Not a hierarchy where man dominates woman to the point of oppression, but a caring and loving relationship where the man takes responsibility for the governing of the home, while the woman supports and nurtures the same.

We often hear ecologists talk about the "biosphere," the world environment that must be protected. If one small part of that biosphere is destroyed, it affects the whole. Likewise, when men and women tamper with what God has created, the order of society changes—for the worse. The increase in out-of-wedlock births, sexually transmitted diseases and divorce are a testimony to man trying to second guess his Creator.

The biblical admonition of "children obey your parents" (Ephesians 6:1) has also been discarded. The children, however, are not the problem here, for it is the parents who are to discipline a child and set the borders of proper behavior. Twenty first century society has put so much emphasis on letting children "explore and develop their full potential" on their own, that respect for authority, and age, have been neglected—or scorned. Proverbs 21:6 is often quoted in this regard; parents are to "train up a child" so when he is "old he will not depart." The idea is to instill proper behavior and morals so that the child will instinctively know what is right as he grows older. However, the Hebrew text is open to another interpretation. This one says that training a child in "the way he should go" refers to the parent letting the child do what he or she pleases. As a result, the child will grow to have a self-centered and immature view of the world.

The pagan worldview is not only blasphemous in content, it is simply *immature*; pagans are children that have been left to the abandonment of their own view of what is right and wrong. As such, they are in rebellion against a holy God who has created all we see, and who has set up expectations of behavior, the most important of which is belief and submission to His Son, who died a vicarious death for sinners.

The Gospel gives Christians the hope and promise to carry on in a world antithetical to the guidelines put in place by God. It is the fuel and the balm needed to renew the soul, and to inspire courage. Even in the face of adversity, the Gospel triumphs. What passes for persecution in the American church, would not so much as get a second look in the church in China. The apostle Paul saw his persecution, even his imprisonment, as an ally in the preaching of the Gospel:

> *Philippians 1: 12-14 But I want you to know, brethren, that the things which happened to me have actually turned out for the furtherance of the gospel, so that it has become evident to the whole palace guard, and to all the rest, that my chains are in Christ; and most of the brethren in the Lord, having become confident by my chains, are much more bold to speak the word without fear.*

Persecution is the well from which the church renews its strength, and carries on the battle.

FIFTEEN
More Than Conquerors

THE BIBLE CONSISTENTLY TELLS CHRISTIANS to set their minds on the things "above"; on heavenly things pertaining to salvation, not the things of this earth (Colossians 3:2). Yet, they are also responsible for how they behave here on earth; how they relate to those in authority and to their neighbors (Romans 13:1-10).

Certainly, it would be an act of irresponsibility for Christians to live in a fallen world and not proclaim the gospel; they are, in fact, commanded to do so. Christians are never told in Scripture to take over the government and establish a theocracy. Rather, they are told to be ambassadors for Christ, pleading with a lost world to turn to the Savior (2 Corinthians 5:20). Christians have been justified by the blood of Christ (Romans 5:9) and are now called to live accordingly. By doing so, that is, by living a Christ-like life that is much different than the culture around them, their influence will be felt. This is not to say that Christians should live an ascetic lifestyle; they are not told to do this either (cf. Galatians). Instead, they are to be good citizens by being good examples. They must portray to the culture around them the paradigm of life as God intends it to be.

Christian history has certainly been marred by excesses, and even out right brutality. But we live in a fallen creation, and even Christians are subject to the pull of the flesh. The apostle Paul said that what he truly wanted to do he "did not practice; but what I hate, that I do" (Romans 7:15). Critics of the Christian faith have always, and will always, point to certain times in the course of history where Christians have failed to live up to the standard set by God. Try as they might, however, they cannot deny the positive influence that Christians have had on the world in all areas of human endeavor. Even in the world today, Christian acts of mercy far surpass the politically motivated charity of a United Nations—and seem to be much more efficient.

More to the point, Christians are called to be the light in a very dark world. They are not to be in retreat as the prevailing pagan culture closes in. They are, in fact, to ever be moving forward.

In Matthew 16:18, Jesus tells us that the "gates of hell shall not prevail" against the church. Most Christians have the mind picture of the minions of hell, pouring over the church's barricade, as gallant Christians push them back from whence they came. But this is not the image Christ is giving us in this passage. Rather, it is of a victorious and aggressive church making a full frontal assault on the very gates of hell! The church is not commanded to be a passive entity in the world, but a vibrant and living organism, bringing new life to whomever it touches.

The aforementioned, of course, is applicable to the theme of this book: the transformation of culture. When we say "transformation," we are not necessarily saying that the culture at large will be overtly Christian; that it will have a fully Christian government, or make a particular brand of Christianity the official state church. But we are saying that certain standards will be apparent to all to both edify believers and restrain the destructive behavior of unbelievers. Let us take for example, America in the 1950's. Certainly, not everybody was a church-going believer, but there was an agreed upon behavior pattern that most observed: respect for adults and authority, for the Bible—even if one did not fully subscribe to it—and a generally favorable disposition to patriotism.

Simply compare that with today's model and the reality becomes apparent, whether we consider divorce, out-of-wedlock births, sexually transmitted diseases, violence against parents or violent crime. Material on this subject is quite copious, and we will not repeat it here. However, the facts do speak for themselves.

Has, therefore, the Gospel lost ground? If societal mores are sliding, seemingly, into the abyss, is this not an indictment upon the church? If the Gospel is the power to save, why is it not redeeming contemporary western society?

The answer to this is not a simple one. True, American culture has become a *lack* of culture, but the progress of the Gospel is not always overtly apparent. The number of weekly conversions and baptisms are not usually broadcast on the nightly news—nor is the number of families that have been brought back together and emotionally healed by the preaching of the Gospel. So one would be hard pressed to make a definitive assessment of how much ground has been gained or lost. What's more, to put everything in the context of the American church would be a gross mistake.

Consider, for example, the fact that less than twenty years ago, getting the Gospel into Eastern Europe was virtually impossible. Indeed, Albania under Enver Hoxha had a standing order to immediately execute anyone caught with a Bible, while neighboring countries had severe, if less radical, ways of dealing with the church. With the fall of the Berlin wall, however, and Eastern Europe's need to turn to a market economy, those societies once so closed to the west simply could not get enough of Western culture. This opened these countries to tourism, and to a freer exchange of cultural ideas. Because of this, missionaries, if not being openly welcomed, were at least allowed to labor in the Gospel.

Technology has also played a big part in evangelism. Satellites can now beam the message of the Gospel via radio, TV or the Internet.

Many struggling for basic human rights under authoritarian regimes are Christian believers who attempt to bring non-violent change to their country. The Christian "underground" in many of these countries are responsible for incredible acts of courage as they work with the poor and those seeking to practice their faith apart from government interference.

The great plan of salvation that God has bestowed on the world is like a fine diamond; as we look at it from various angles its unique beauty simply dazzles us. That God in Christ Jesus would create one culture from the various nations is no small miracle. Christians feel an instant bond to other believers who may not even share their language or native culture. They are united into one culture, a superior culture of many shapes and colors, all proclaiming the glorious work of Christ, to a lost and dying world.

www.ingramcontent.com/pod-product-compliance
Lightning Source LLC
Chambersburg PA
CBHW032129090426
42743CB00007B/533